Dedicated To:

Southern Baptist missionary, James Turner, who laid down his life for the Gospel and for me. He was killed by Muslim fanatics because he dared to baptize me in the Arabian Sea soon after I received Jesus Christ and came out of Islam.

Danyel Jones, my teammate and co-laborer, who laid down her life in the service of the Gospel in Africa. Her blood that stained the soil of Africa cries out to us who remain, that we continue to press forward with this precious Blood-bought Gospel that is entrusted to us by God.

> *"When you go home, tell them of us and say,*
> *for their tomorrow, we gave our today."*
> -J M Edmonds

All Things
are
Possible

Eyewitness accounts of true miracles of Jesus Christ

Christopher Alam

All Things Are Possible
ISBN-13: 978-0-8920177-0-8
ISBN-10: 0-8920177-0-7

Copyright © 2010 Christopher Alam
All Rights Reserved
Printed in the USA
Third printing, 2010

Dynamis World Ministries
aka Christopher Alam Ministries International
2384 New Holland Pike
Lancaster, Pa 17601, USA
Tel: 717.656.0362   Fax: 717.390.0363
www.pentecostalfire.com
info@pentecostalfire.com

Cover photo: Istockphoto.com
Cover design: Jan Davis

Contents

Foreword

In Christopher Alam's latest book, *"All Things Are Possible,"* you will find detailed, heart-stirring testimonies of people who have been supernaturally healed and touched by the power of the Almighty God. This extra boost of faith packed within this book is set on a strong foundation of faith in Jesus, who is "the same yesterday, today and forever"! Often in life, we find it easy to look to methods and others to change our circumstances. However, this book takes us back to the basics, and reminds us that Jesus is our source for all good things.

Having preached the gospel for 32 years, Christopher Alam has seen the power of God working in over 70 nations in the world. As you read the true accounts of commonplace and even "unusual" miracles, you will be awestruck and deeply convicted that your faith in Jesus always works! As Christopher Alam puts it, "When Jesus walks in, every equation...changes. One plus one is suddenly greater than a million; impossibilities are suddenly not impossibilities anymore...because with Him all things are possible!" Your faith in Christ can overcome all things!

Pastor Kong Hee, Senior Pastor, City Harvest Church
Singapore

Comments

"*Reading 'All Things are Possible' brings a fresh hunger for the mighty workings of the power of God. Get ready to read Acts, the 29th chapter. Jesus truly is the same yesterday, today and forever and has shown Himself alive in Christopher's life and ministry.*"

John Nuzzo, Senior Pastor, Victory Family Church
Cranberry Township, Pennsylvania

"*This book will cause your faith to increase, to truly believe that 'All Things Are Possible.' As God has anointed and used Christopher Alam to see the miracles of the Book of Acts come alive today, may your faith increase to believe the same for yourself, your family, your friends and your city.*"

Paul E. Grabill, Senior Pastor, State College Assembly of God
State College, Pennsylvania

"*I was personally challenged and encouraged by "All Things Are Possible." The stories of God's miracle working power in action often moved me to tears. My prayer is that this book will enlarge your faith and increase your expectation for greater evidences of the power of Jesus in your life.*"

Jeff Leake, Senior Pastor, Allison Park Church
Pittsburgh, Pennsylvania

"The Gift of Helps: In I Corinthians 12 are listed spiritual gifts God has set in the church. One of those gifts is called 'the gift of helps.' My friend, Christopher Alam, manifests this wonderful gift all over the world. Other gifts flow through him---the gifts of healing, the working of miracles among others. In my teaming with him in Burma for dynamic ministry, I have praised God for this 'gift of helps' I've observed at close hand. Once he insisted I take his first class airline ticket while he kindly chose to take my seat in the economy section. His impact upon his team demonstrates repeatedly the generosity that motivates his life."

Reverend Don Gossett, Bold Bible Missions
Blaine, Washington

Prologue

"Now when John had heard in the prison the works of Christ, he sent two of his disciples, And said unto him, Art thou he that should come, or do we look for another? Jesus answered and said unto them, Go and shew John again those things which ye do hear and see: The blind receive their sight, and the lame walk, the lepers are cleansed, and the deaf hear, the dead are raised up, and the poor have the gospel preached to them." Matthew 11:2-5

I am writing this book to share with you, the reader, about some of the wonderful things that I have seen God do before my very eyes. The purpose of this book is twofold: firstly to acknowledge and to give glory to God our Heavenly Father through our Lord Jesus Christ. It is He alone who can do such wonders, and He alone is worthy of all glory, honor and praise. Secondly, that you who read this may be blessed and be encouraged in your own faith by the testimonies related here. This being said, I must also state that books like this can merely encourage us to a certain extent; and that there is only one book, the Bible, the infallible Word of God, that can impart life, faith and power unto us!

Whilst reading this book, please do not at any time forget that I, the writer, am an ordinary man. Please remember that these accounts are about the works of the Lord Jesus Christ, rather than those of a man.

I am merely a broken vessel for the Glory of God. I cannot boast of ever having done anything great in my life, nor have I ever achieved or accomplished anything that could be deemed as remarkable or significant in any way. I have just been blessed to have been present at the right time and in the right place where our Lord Jesus has chosen to manifest His power; yes, in this I do admit that I have received far more than I could have ever deserved in this life. Yes, ever since that day when I came out of Islam to our Lord Jesus Christ, God, because of the unfathomable depths of His Grace, has always shown His goodness, kindness, mercy and favor to me far more than I ever could have imagined, thought of or asked for.

So once again I say, with all my heart:

"All glory, honor and praise to our Lord Jesus, because He, and He alone is Worthy!"

Christopher Alam

Chapter 1

JESUS HAS NEVER CHANGED!

The Word of God tells us about our Lord Jesus:

> *"And whithersoever he entered, into villages, or cities, or country, they laid the sick in the streets, and besought him that they might touch if it were but the border of his garment: and as many as touched him were made whole."* Mark 6:56

O, what a wonderful Savior. The people living in those days knew that Jesus was the source of life and healing. That is why they came to Him, knowing that if they would only touch His garments as He passed by, they would be healed; and they were!

My Bible also says,

> *"Jesus Christ the same yesterday, and to day, and for ever."* Hebrews 13:8

This Jesus who the people touched then is still the same today. Even today, those who touch Him are healed just as the people were in the days when He physically walked upon this earth.

Everything in the world changes, but God never changes. His Word never changes. The writ of His infallible and eternal Word says the same thing today as it always has throughout history. God and His Word are for ever steadfast and unchanging. He Himself declares,

> *"I am the LORD, I change not."* Malachi 3:6

Jesus Christ is still the same yesterday, today and for ever. He is still the Healer. Our God is still a God of miracles. He still heals the sick and sets free those that are bound or tormented by the powers of darkness. The world changes, churches change their beliefs, theologians, and preachers expound on why it is not realistic for us to expect miracles from God anymore; but in spite of all this, Jesus never changes. He still remains the same.

As I write this book, I look back through the years at the past, to the greatest miracle that I have ever personally experienced in my own life. It was the day in December 1975 when Jesus came into my heart and saved me from a sinful life and transformed me.

> *"Therefore if any man be in Christ, he is a new creature: old things are passed away; behold, all things are become new. And all things are of God, who hath reconciled us to himself by Jesus Christ."* 2 Corinthians 5:17-18

That, in my eyes, is the greatest miracle that God can do for man; when He saves and transforms the heart of a sinner, taking away the old and making all things new. I was lost and dying, without hope and on my way to spending eternity in Hell far away from the presence of God. Then Jesus came and touched me and changed my eternal destiny. This was just as God promised, *"And I will give them one heart, and I will put a new spirit within you; and I will take the stony heart out of their*

2

flesh, and will give them a heart of flesh" (Ezekiel 11:19).

Three days after that momentous day when I first met the Living Christ, I was handing out gospel tracts to people on the streets. I then heard the voice of God for the first time in my life. It was clear, audible. The Voice said, "This is what you shall do for the rest of your life. I shall take you all around the world, and you shall tell people about Jesus!"

Understanding that this was my destiny and calling by God, I decided to obey and follow God's bidding.

At the time of writing, in 2008, I have preached the Gospel for over 32 years and have seen Jesus change the lives of millions of people in over 70 nations of the world. I have seen Him do for millions of others that which He did for me. I have also had the priceless privilege of seeing Him do innumerable and wonderful works of healing and deliverance from diseases and from evil spirits. I have seen God raise up the dead and make hopelessly paralyzed and crippled people get up and walk. I have seen Him open blind eyes, create missing body parts, straighten twisted deformed bodies and make those born deaf and mute hear and speak. I have seen hopelessly insane and demon-possessed people totally set free and restored by the power of the Lord Jesus Christ.

This is the God who I serve!

I know by the Word of God and by the things that I have seen that our Lord Jesus is alive today. He has never changed. His power, love, mercy and compassion are still the same.

We live in an age when man is very proud of his achievements and the advancements that he has made in different fields of science and knowledge. World leaders and the sages of this age talk about a better world, but in spite of all this more wars are being fought today than in the ages past, using weapons far more horrific than the ordinary person can imagine or comprehend. There are great advances in medicine, yet there are terrible and deadly diseases today that did not exist before, and man finds himself powerless before these diseases. Not only this, but there is also gross darkness in the heart of man such has never been seen before.

All this shows that man, at the height of his knowledge and abilities, is less than nothing. He can send a spaceship to Mars but cannot deal with the evil in his own heart. Man at his very best, at the very acme of his abilities, falls far short of the glory of God. From that low place of sin and nothingness, when man comes to the end of self and calls out to God, God comes in. And what is God's answer to man's cry? He loved unlovable mankind so much that He sent his only son Jesus to bear all of mankind's sin, diseases, infirmities and torments upon His own self when He died upon the Cross of Calvary.

> *"But He was wounded for our transgressions, He was bruised for our iniquities. The chastisement of our peace was upon Him, and by His stripes we are healed."*
> Isaiah 53:5

Then after three days this Jesus was raised up from the dead by the power of God the Father. He is alive today; the Savior, Healer, and Giver of life to everybody who comes to God through Him.

God's order and pattern is that His healing power should always follow the preaching of His Gospel. That is why, whenever and wherever I have preached the Gospel, God has always confirmed His Word with signs, wonders, and miracles. Miracles should always follow the preaching of the

Gospel message; that is the Biblical pattern. Take for example our crusades in Africa. From 1987 to the time of writing in September 2008, I have held about 150 crusades in Africa with about 6 services in each crusade. That is 900 services in total with huge multitudes present at each service. In all these years I have never seen a single service without significant miracles taking place. We have NEVER ended a service saying, "Well, I guess it wasn't God's will to heal anybody tonight." This is because God always stands behind the Gospel message that presents His Son Jesus Christ as the Savior of sinners.

This is not about how anointed preachers are, but about how wonderful, how full of compassion, mercy, and power Jesus is. The truth is that we who preach the Gospel are nothing in ourselves. We are earthen vessels carrying the Glory of God, all because of His Grace bestowed upon us.

"But we have this treasure in earthen vessels, that the excellency of the power may be of God, and not of us."
2 Corinthians 4:7

We are ordinary men called and anointed by God, used by Him. God's calling upon our lives is not based upon our merits, but because it pleased Him to choose those that are weak and nothing in themselves.

"But God hath chosen the foolish things of the world to confound the wise; and God hath chosen the weak things of the world to confound the things which are mighty; And base things of the world, and things which are despised, hath God chosen, yea, and things which are not, to bring to nought things that are: That no flesh should glory in his presence." 1 Corinthians 1:27-29

Let us always remember this! If it were not for God's Grace upon our lives, where would we be? God's servants come and go, but the Gospel of Jesus is perpetual, eternal. It was, is and always shall remain the most powerful Force in the universe. When the Gospel is preached, the Father is exalted, Jesus is manifested and the Holy Ghost shows His power. Sinful men are saved, demons are cast out and the diseased are healed. This is the power of the Gospel, as the Apostle Paul said, *"The glorious gospel of the blessed God"* (1 Timothy 1:11).

God heals "small" things like headaches, and He also does "big" things like making the lame to walk. "Big" miracles or "small", they are all miracles. Sometimes there are multitudes of miracles, like in the final service of our first crusade in Lashio, Burma, where amongst others, over 225 deaf people were instantly healed and 12 lame people got up and walked.

There are at times very unusual miracles, like what God did for a tall lanky Masai tribesman who showed up one evening at our crusade in Iringa, Tanzania. He had only one eye, and where the other eye should have been was a gaping empty socket. When we prayed for the crowd *en masse*, God touched him and created a new eye in the empty socket. God did something similar to a lady in Kalaymyo, Burma whose eye had been pierced and destroyed by a bamboo arrow. As she stood in the crowd, God created a new eye for her.

Then there was the little girl in one of the townships outside Lusaka, Zambia. She was carried to the crusade by her father. She had only one normal arm, the left arm being a small and deformed little extremity about six inches long. When the power of God fell upon the vast crowd that night, the little extremity began to grow out. The people watching this screamed and shouted as it happened. They watched how first an arm formed and then grew out to full length; then a hand and fingers grew out until it became a perfectly normal and functioning limb. It is mind-boggling, hard to

6

even imagine, but such are the things that our Lord Jesus Christ can do!

Does it sound incredulous? To be honest, my mind cannot understand or keep up with such things either. I have witnessed God do things that my limited human mind has been totally unable to take in, even after I have seen them happen before my very eyes.

Strange things? Well, it can get stranger still! I remember a lady in Lashio, Burma, who was born totally blind. Her eyeballs were white orbs, with no pupils. The amazing thing was that even after God healed her, she still had no pupils in her eyes. Her eyes were still white orbs, yet she could see perfectly! Then there was the Indian man in Rangoon, Burma, who was born without an ear. The place where the ear is normally located was flat and smooth like his cheek; there wasn't even an aperture there. God healed him, but did not create an ear for the man. The man could now hear perfectly even though there was no ear there!

Then there is the amazing story of a deaf-mute man who came to our crusade in Lubumbashi in Congo. This man was born without both ears. He had never heard a sound nor had he ever spoken a word in his entire life. Jesus healed him and he began to hear and to speak. My friend, Pastor David Newberry, a Pentecostal missionary with over 35 years in Africa, was with me. He got excited and walked over to the man along with a Congolese interpreter/pastor. Just imagine Pastor Newberry's shock when this man who had never heard nor spoken before spoke to him in perfect West Texas English (David Newberry is from West Texas)! The man then turned to the Congolese pastor and addressed him in perfect French. Amazing, considering the fact that he had been totally deaf and mute all his life! But then again, we are talking about our wonderful Lord Jesus here, the One who does things far more amazing than we can ever imagine… *"For with God nothing shall be impossible."* Luke 1:37

These things go beyond the scope of man's understanding. Thank God that we serve Jesus by faith and not by sight, otherwise what would we do, we creatures of limited understanding called to serve such an omnipotent and all-knowing God?

Sometimes miracles generate expectation in other people, causing a release of God's power into or through their lives. This is what happened in a township outside of Lusaka, Zambia, where we held a crusade a few years ago. It was daytime and a group of young men from the local churches who we had employed as security men were guarding our crusade equipment. There was a family nearby whose little baby was seriously ill. The husband had gone to work and the wife was home caring for the sick child. It was around 10 in the morning. The child died during that time. People in African countries, most unfortunately, do not readily have access to emergency medical services as in the US and in Europe. The poor family did not have a telephone either. At the baby's death the mother panicked and became totally hysterical. Screaming and crying she ran out of the house carrying her dead baby. Across the soccer field she came, running straight to our preaching platform. She left the baby there wrapped up in a blanket and ran away into the distance crying hysterically.

Our security men were taken by surprise. They looked to check the contents of the bundle that the woman had left behind. Imagine their surprise when they discovered that it was a dead baby; the body cold and stiff. They were shocked. What should they do? Then one of them said to the others, "Look, we have seen miracles here every night, and we all have heard what Pastor Christopher always says, that Jesus is the same today and that we should always expect great things from God!"

So they gathered around the dead baby and began to pray, sing, praise, and worship God. People began to gather and watch, and they kept on singing, praying, and worshiping God for a long time. Then suddenly the dead baby began to stir and to cry. Somebody picked the baby up; the people, who hitherto had been curious onlookers, joined in. They began to dance, shout and praise God. One of the security men began to preach the gospel to the crowd, and gave an altar call for people to receive Jesus Christ. Another ran to buy some milk for the baby. By the time he came back with the milk, the people in that crowd who had witnessed this wonderful miracle had all received Jesus Christ as their Lord and Savior.

The baby's father returned from work late in the afternoon. Then at around 4 pm, he, his wife and their relatives came to fetch the body of the dead baby. Imagine their joy when they found out that their baby had been raised up from the dead and was alive because of the power of the Lord Jesus Christ!

They, too, then gave their lives to Jesus.

This is a true story, an example of what Jesus can do. This is what the Gospel of Jesus is all about: God's love and compassion for man. Jesus Christ the Son of God saving sinners, touching people, healing and raising them up, and setting them free.

In the last service of a crusade in Zambia in March 2007, I saw a little girl who had never sat, stood nor walked since birth, get up and walk across the platform before a huge multitude of people. The noise was deafening as the people cheered and shouted, praising God. In the midst of all this, my eyes fell on the child's mother. She stood at the end of the platform with her hands on her face, weeping profusely, tears flowing down her brown cheeks, looking at her daughter walking. She was broken before God, o so deeply thankful, unable even to say anything except just weep…

The next evening, I was on a plane flying back home. My thoughts went back to the last service, to the sight of that little girl walking for the first time in her life… My mind was still trying to come to grips with the astounding miracle that my eyes had witnessed.

I pondered within myself, "How can such things happen?" In my mind I replayed every detail of the scene from the previous evening. I was there upon the platform before that vast crowd; a man unworthy in my own flesh, and with my unworthy lips I had called upon the worthy and Holy Name of Jesus Christ of Nazareth, the Son of God. At the mention of that most glorious of all names, God in Heaven had sent His Spirit, His Life and Power into that crippled and paralyzed little body. As the power of God surged through her body, it had been straightened up, totally healed; she had then stood up and begun to walk. It was because of that Name that I had spoken; the wonderful Name of Jesus. O, that worthy Name! That Name that is above every other name, at the mention of which every knee has to bow!

O, that God had counted me worthy to speak that precious Name. I wept, realizing what a high privilege God had bestowed upon me; that I who was unworthy in my self was counted worthy because of the Blood of Jesus, and that as His child and servant I had the right to speak the Name of Jesus that destroys all the works of Satan.

"And his name through faith in his name hath made this man strong, whom ye see and know: yea, the faith which

is by him hath given him this perfect soundness in the presence of you all." Acts 3:16

I have written this book to share with you, the reader, a few such true stories of the wonderful things that I have seen God do over the years.

This is an age of lawyers, disclaimers, lawsuits, and such, and so I must say this: Working in primitive conditions in third-world countries, I do not have access to medical records or physicians' certificates for these testimonies. All I can say is that each one of these stories is true to the best of my knowledge, and that these events took place in the presence of many Christian witnesses. To me, such things are priceless beyond all the wealth of this world, but God in His Grace gives these freely to all those who ask Him. It is time for us to rise up in faith and appropriate every blessing that Jesus has purchased for us through His Blood.

What a wonderful Jesus we serve!

I have many other such stories to tell, but I have chosen a few here to share with you. I am doing this for the glory of God, to give honor and glory and praise to our wonderful Lord Jesus, for He alone is worthy! I am also doing this to encourage you who need a miracle from God, that you may see that for you too, "all things are possible!"

Look up! Do not give up! Hold on to the horns of the Altar! Believe in God for your miracle! My prayer is that God would use this book to touch your heart and cause you to draw even closer to our Lord Jesus. He loves you so much that He died for you, bearing upon Himself all your sins and diseases. He rose up from death to be your Savior, Healer, and Deliverer.

11

All Things are Possible

Chapter 2

RESURRECTION POWER
A DEAD MAN RAISED!

BURMA

This wonderful miracle took place in an indoor crusade service that I held in Rangoon in Burma in the late 90s. To tell this story more fully I must first briefly tell the story of a girl called Lin Lin Tun, a Burmese teenager. She was only 17 at that time and a new Christian who had only recently come to Jesus out of Buddhism. When she told her family about her faith in Jesus, they had responded by throwing her out of the house. She had nowhere to go, so we had taken her in. She lived and studied at a Bible school run by friends of mine.

I remembered how, as a new Christian, I had gone through the very same rejection from my family that Lin Lin was now experiencing; so my heart went out to her. I had, more or less, "adopted" her as a daughter. Lin Lin and I were very close; she called me "Papa," and everybody referred to her as my daughter. In fact, when my Burmese friends decided to give me a Burmese name, it was *Shwe Kyar Tun Lin*, so that it would match her name, Lin Lin Tun. My Burmese name, Shwe Kyar Tun Lin, means "The Golden Tiger that Shines Brightly." Lin Lin was on fire for Jesus with a burning zeal for the Gospel. She was always eager to learn and followed

13

me everywhere, steadfastly standing beside me when I would minister to the sick.

It was an evening service and many sick people were being brought to the front for prayer. In the throng, I noticed a deathly ill middle-aged man being carried to the front by some people. He was extremely weak, wasted and skeletal, and looked like he was in the final stages of some terrible diseases, just a mere whisper away from death. The people who had brought him were propping him up. I was praying for some other people with Lin Lin by my side. Suddenly, as I watched, the man breathed his last and died, his body sliding lifelessly to the floor.

There were some physicians and nurses present at the meeting. They left their seats and rushed to the front and proceeded to examine the lifeless form on the floor. Yes, they confirmed, the man was indeed dead. I then expected these trained medical professionals to get into action and work feverishly to try to bring the man back to life, just like I had seen it done so many times in television shows. But that never happened. Instead, they did something that I found most bizarre and surreal; they all quietly got up from beside the dead man on the floor and went back to their seats! There they sat silently, watching me, expecting me to do something about the dead body that lay between the pews and the platform.

I was numb with surprise and shock, never having seen anyone actually die in a service. With some quick thinking I figured that there was really only one of two things that we could do: Bury him or raise him up from the dead.

For a Pentecostal like me the choice was obvious. This was a Holy Ghost meeting, and asking God to raise the dead man would be the most proper and appropriate thing to do. The only problem was that I did not know how to raise the dead. I had never seen it done before nor had any of my teachers in the two Bible schools that I had attended ever taught me how to do it.

"Raising the dead" was not part of the curriculum.

Not really knowing what to do next, I stood by the lifeless form of the man, with Lin Lin beside me. We looked at the dead man, and then I remembered something that I had learned from a preacher many years ago, that when we do not know what to do, the Holy Ghost always knows; and that the best thing to do is to pray in the Holy Ghost.

We began to pray in other tongues. The presence of death is a very dark and depressive thing that can have a paralyzing effect upon one's faith. It casts a heavy shadow that quenches faith, and we first have to rise above it before God can move on our behalf. God cannot work when we allow ourselves to go under the dark clouds of a depressive atmosphere of death, darkness and unbelief. We are creatures that thrive in the Light of God and should always pray ourselves out of the dark shadows of death into an atmosphere of Jesus, faith, life, light, and victory.

We continued to pray in other tongues to break through the heavy pall of darkness that surrounded us. In situations like this, quiet Charismatic bedroom prayers do not work. One has to pray with power and get really fervent; "generate some heat," so as to say. So, we prayed loudly in the Holy Ghost.

As we kept on in prayer, I felt after some time that our hearts were being lifted up in Jesus, above the depressive shadows of death. We kept pressing on in prayer. The presence of Jesus was now becoming more and more tangible. The spirit of life arose and grew bigger in the room, and the spirit of death became correspondingly smaller and its hold began to diminish. We were breaking through! Then I began to feel the Fire of the Holy Ghost. We began to shout. Any full-blooded Fire-Baptized Pentecostal would know what I am talking about. The Fire of God sends something like shivers, tingling and flames coursing through the body from head to toe. Once you have been touched by the Fire of God you can never truly enjoy a dead religious setting any more, where the Holy Ghost does not move with power. It is not mere emotion, but so much more than that. It is something that takes hold of us and moves us to shout, pray, dance, be wild about Jesus, and speak the Word of God in victory.

With our hands lifted up to God, we prayed louder and louder, shouting, pressing on to the very Throne of God. Not knowing how or what to pray, we prayed in tongues. At one time, I opened my eyes and looked at Lin Lin. A stream of tears rolled down her face as she cried out to God, praying for the dead man. On her face, I could see compassion, brokenness; her face shone like the face of an angel. I knew that she had taken hold of the horns of the altar and was storming the very Throne of God!

To see the Glory of God upon my daughter's face inspired me, lifted me up; and we pressed right into the Holy Presence of God. I do not know exactly how long we prayed; but we were shouting out the Word of God, calling upon the name of the Lord, proclaiming His victory over death, speaking forth life to come into the dead body, storming the very Throne of God. It can best be described as it is written in the Word of God, *"The kingdom of heaven suffereth violence, and the violent take it by force"* (Matthew 11:12).

Suddenly, I heard a very loud and deafening, "HALLELUJAH!" that rang and echoed through the room.

16

Startled, I opened my eyes and saw a flash of movement before my face. It was the dead man. The resurrection power of our Lord Jesus had touched him. It had hit him and had literally lifted him right off the floor. He had shot straight up into the air like a rocket, his feet coming off the ground. On his way up he had lifted his hands up to God and shouted the loud "Hallelujah" that had so startled me. He then landed squarely upon his feet, worshiping, shouting, and praising God.

The whole crowd stood to their feet and erupted into praise, weeping, shouting, and worshiping God.

Lin Lin and I were overwhelmed and broken in God's Presence. Our shouting turned into brokenness and tears of joy. We felt so broken, unworthy even to stand there; yet in Jesus we were overwhelmed and thankful to be so blessed by God, to be there to see His Power and His Glory. The crowd was shouting, and we were prostrate on the floor, weeping.

Was there any spiritual "procedure," "formula" or "method" that we had followed in order to see this dead man raised to life? No, none whatsoever. It was Jesus and Jesus alone. The Life that is in Jesus is greater than all the death in this world. Lin Lin and I were privileged to be there with Jesus when He brought the dead man back to life. It was a demonstration of the resurrection power of our blessed Savior, who alone is worthy of all glory, honor, and praise.

Can I now write a manual on how to raise the dead? No. All I know is that our Lord Jesus was there, and that He is the same today as He always has been through the ages. His love and His power are undiminished and still remain the same. We should never give up, even in the face of death itself; because the power of Jesus Christ is far greater than even the power of death. If we live our lives in expectations of great things from God, if we believe and let the Spirit of God carry us, we shall always see the Glory of God.

"Heal the sick, cleanse the lepers, raise the dead, cast out devils: freely ye have received, freely give." Matthew 10:8

Our Lord Jesus, and not Satan, holds the keys to death (Revelation 1:18). Satan no longer decides when our lives should end; that prerogative now belongs to Jesus. He says, *"With long life will I satisfy him, and shew him my salvation"* (Psalm 91:16).

That is God's plan for you!

Jesus has triumphed over death and won total victory. His Name is mighty even to bring people back from the dead. With God nothing is impossible!

Chapter 3

THE PARALYZED MAN
BIALKA, POLAND

It was July 1983. My wife, Britta, and I had graduated from RHEMA Bible Training Center in Broken Arrow, Oklahoma, the year before and we now lived in Linkoping in Sweden. We had started a small Bible School and I also itinerated in churches on the weekends. We knew that God had called us to overseas missions and were waiting for Him to open the right doors for us to step out into missions work.

The phone rang one afternoon. It was Borje Eliasson, a dear friend of mine from the West coast of Sweden. He told me that he and his wife Ragni along with another couple, Evert and Bittan Hedin, were taking a large supply of food down to a Roman Catholic students' camp in Southern Poland. He wondered whether I would be interested in accompanying them on the trip. My share of the expenses would be around $100; I talked to Britta and found out that $100 was all that we had in the bank, just enough to enable me to go with my friends to Poland.

Britta and I prayed about it, and we both felt that this was what we had been waiting for; this was God's "open door" through which we would step out into foreign missions.

I was excited because this would be my first ever trip to Communist-ruled Eastern Europe. I had only recently become a Swedish citizen, and had traded in my United Nations Geneva Convention Refugees Travel Document (Also known by the fancier name of "Passeport L'Etranger") for a shiny new black Swedish passport. Sweden was a neutral country, not allied with either side in the Cold War. Because of this, it was easy for Swedish subjects to get visas for travel to communist countries. I could therefore quickly and without any problems get a visa to visit Poland.

Poland was then under the iron fist of a communist military government that ruled by martial law. Things were very difficult for the Poles and they had acute shortages of everything, including basics such as food and medicines. People had to stand in line to buy even the most basic necessities such as bread and meat. A Polish friend of mine, a university professor, told me that he often stood in line for 12 hours at a time just to buy a loaf of bread or a few sausages.

We were taking our shipment of food down to a large summer camp that Charismatic Catholic monks from the main Dominican church in Krakow were holding for students from the University of Krakow. This camp, held by the Catholic "Oasis - Light and Life" movement, was being held in the village of Bialka, not far from the picturesque ski resort town of Zakopane in the Carpathian Mountains of Southern Poland.

We arrived in Bialka after three days of driving across Sweden and Poland plus an overnight ferry crossing the Baltic Sea. We decided to spend the whole week there with the monks and the students at the camp. They were most grateful for the food that we had brought, and out of courtesy asked if there was anything that we wanted to do.

Before anybody could say anything, I jumped up and said, "Yes, I want to preach to your students!"

They did not know me, but yet most graciously agreed to let me minister to the students, even though I was Pentecostal and not Roman Catholic like they were. I preached to different groups of students every evening. God moved in these meetings and we saw each and every student present in the meetings receive Jesus and get baptized with the Holy Ghost. Many were also healed from different diseases and infirmities. Most of the monks rejoiced over what the Lord was doing in our midst but some of them appeared to be somewhat perplexed about what was taking place. It turned out that they were holding a special 7-week Charismatic Catholic "Life in the Spirit" course for the students. The course was supposed to lead them into salvation and finally culminate with the laying on of hands for the Baptism with the Holy Ghost on the last day of the 7th week. Now I had come in and unwittingly turned their plans upside-down; everybody had already received Christ and they were all speaking in tongues only a week into the 7 week course!

Bialka is a small rural village, and we were quartered in a log cabin in a pig farm that stank to high heaven; I had never been in such a foul-smelling place in my entire life. There were no beds in the cabin, so the two couples and I slept in sleeping bags on the floor, all together in one tiny room. The entire area was very primitive; there were no televisions, radios, newspapers, or even a shop where we could buy sodas or snacks. On top of this, nobody spoke any English except our interpreter. Father Joakim, one of the older monks, spoke some Swedish because his mother was Swedish. We were awakened daily at the crack of dawn by millions of flies that would invade and literally fill up the tiny room that the five of us shared. The flies were unbearable, and in order to keep my sanity I would

21

get up early before dawn, wash up and go outside into the surrounding fields and orchards to walk around, pray and worship God.

I was not used to being in places where there was nothing to do when it came to entertainment and such. With nothing else to do but preach in the evenings, walking around worshiping God became my way of passing the time and also escaping the flies and the boredom. I would spend many hours with Jesus every day, from morning till evening, fellowshipping with Him, enjoying His presence and praying in the Spirit. After a couple of days, I sensed a change, a transformation beginning to take place in my inner man. My mind was becoming less and less cluttered with the thoughts and the things of this world, and I was more and more at peace within and at rest in my heart and my soul. I found myself waking up very early every morning in anticipation of yet another wonderful day with Jesus. As the day would pass, His gentle voice would speak to me. It was precious, priceless. My heart was full of Jesus and I would literally sense His presence all around me throughout the day. Here I was, walking in the same world as everybody else, but it was as if I lived and breathed in a totally different dimension than the world that surrounded me.

The day before we were to leave to go back to Sweden, I was asked to come and pray for a paralyzed man. He was the father of Maria, one of the leaders of the camp. Maria was engaged to Jacek Reka, the main leader of the camp and of the large Charismatic Catholic group at Krakow University. Her father had been in a serious traffic accident when his car had been broadsided by a large fully loaded truck traveling at high speed. The car had been totally destroyed; he had been flung out of the car and was left paralyzed from his chest down.

Taking along my Swedish friends and a couple of the student leaders, I went to the house where Maria's father lay paralyzed. We were taken to an upstairs bedroom and ushered into a sight of utter hopelessness and despair. The paralyzed man lay on his bed covered by a blanket. He looked hopeless, bewildered, and depressed. He was a skilled motor mechanic, used to physical work, but now he could not even move his body. His whole life had been destroyed by the accident. His poor wife stood next to the bed, her eyes red and swollen by hours of weeping.

Standing beside and looking at the paralyzed figure upon the bed, I felt a sense of total nothingness before God, before man and in the face of the immense suffering before my eyes. What can a man do, or say, faced with such pain and despair? Words failed me and I did not know what to do next. But just then, something happened; I sensed the presence of our Lord Jesus right next to me. My Master, my Lord, my Friend, and constant companion these past days, how could I ever forget that He was always there with me?

The awesome presence of Jesus suddenly filled the room. The hopelessness and despair in that room, until then an insurmountable mountain before me, began to fade away into the shadows. In the presence of Jesus it shrank, withered to nothingness and vanished away.

When Jesus walks in, every equation and mathematical formula changes. One plus one is suddenly greater than a million; impossibilities are suddenly not impossibilities anymore. Jesus was there in that room, and with Him all things are possible.

As I stood by the bedside and looked at the man, still not knowing what to say, words suddenly came pouring out of my mouth. I heard the words, spoken loudly and directed to the paralyzed man, "My brother, fear not, Jesus loves you and God will raise you up!"

I then took out my oil bottle, unscrewed the cap and anointed the paralyzed man in the mighty Name of the Lord Jesus; the Name that stands far above and in power over every single devil, sickness, disease, and infirmity. I then prayed a short prayer of faith. After that, I took his feet and commanded them to receive life and strength from God and to walk. With this done, I stepped back. We all stood still and watched for around 30 or 45 seconds. Then suddenly, the paralyzed man with one sweeping motion threw the blanket off his body and stood up from the bed. With his hands in the air he began to walk around the room, loudly praising God with tears flowing down his face.

We were, first, awestruck and amazed. Then, we suddenly realized the immensity of what the Lord had done before our very eyes. No man had anything to do with it. It was Jesus and Him alone. He was there in the room and He had made this hopelessly paralyzed man whole. We all went down on our faces before God, broken, weeping, and glorifying Him. O, that God had counted us worthy to behold such a miracle! It was wonderful beyond words. We all lay prostrate on the floor and spoke not a word because of the awesome presence of our Savior, whose works are too wonderful for human words to adequately describe.

This miracle opened the way for me to preach the Gospel in Poland. Roman Catholic churches all over the nation threw open their doors to me. For years afterwards, during the remaining dark years of communism, I would regularly and very frequently go to Poland with teams; crisscrossing the country and preaching the Gospel, the Lord confirming His Word with signs following.

I did this until 1990 when I was invited by Polish national TV, in cooperation with the Catholic Church, to preach at a very large church in Gdynia, Poland. Twelve thousand people came every night; 8000 jammed inside the building taking up every available inch of space and a further 4000 standing outside. God did the most amazing miracles and thousands received Jesus. Polish TV then made a 70 minute documentary of this and broadcast it at prime-time. Half of the country's population watched the program, and it touched many lives for Jesus.

When Jesus manifests Himself, when we walk in the consciousness of His precious Presence, all things are possible. Every time I think of this story, I am reminded that it is not really about "methods" or "techniques" of healing, but it is about Jesus and Him alone. When we desire Him, when we seek His presence to walk with Him, the limitations that make certain things "difficult" or "impossible" vanish away. After all, Jesus is the Healer. Jesus is the Miracle Worker and knowing Him intimately and walking with Him is the greatest thing of all. The Apostle Paul had a powerful ministry. He wrote half of the New Testament, planted churches, went up to the Third Heaven, and heard the Voice of God. But, in spite of all these great experiences, the cry of his heart, right up to the end, was nothing else but to know Jesus even better, to be even more like Him.

"That I may know him, and the power of his resurrection, and the fellowship of his sufferings, being made conformable unto his death; If by any means I might attain unto the resurrection of the dead. Not as though I had already attained, either were already perfect: but I follow after, if that I may apprehend that for which also I am apprehended of Christ Jesus." Philippians 3:10-12

Chapter 4

THE PARALYZED BOY
ANGELHOLM, SWEDEN

This wonderful miracle was the first time I ever saw the Lord heal someone who was totally unable to walk. I was working in Uppsala, Sweden, as an evangelist with SESG, the Swedish arm of the Inter-Varsity Fellowship (IVF). I worked under the SESG chaplain at the Uppsala University, a young Lutheran priest called Ulf Ekman, who today pastors the well-known Word of Life Church in Sweden.

There is a background to this story. I was with a group of SESG chaplains, all Lutheran priests, returning home from a staff conference that we had attended in Transtrand, a ski resort up in the mountains of central Sweden. We went to the local railway station to catch the train back home. In fact, everybody in the conference was traveling on that train, heading back to their homes in different cities all over Sweden. As we boarded our assigned carriage and were on our way to our compartment, we passed a few smaller compartments with sleeping berths. The doors of these compartments were all open, and while peeking inside one of these small compartments I saw an elderly lady lying on a berth. She wore gaudy clothes and was heavily made up as if she was on her way home from a party. She looked as if she had passed out drunk.

Like the Pharisees of old, judgmental thoughts immediately came to my mind. "A typical Swedish sinner; she has partied all her life and now she lies there drunk… how disgraceful!" I thought to myself and walked past her onwards to my assigned seat in the main compartment.

I found my seat, and at the exact moment as I was putting my luggage up upon the overhead luggage rack, the Lord spoke to me. He said, "If it was I who passed that woman instead of you, would I have judged her like you just did? What would I do?"

Great conviction came into my heart. I paused and said, "I am sorry Lord Jesus, please forgive me." The Lord then told me to go to the woman and to minister to her. I decided to obey Him immediately. I left my seat and walked back to her compartment, taking a young evangelist along with me. Entering the small sleeping compartment, I noticed that she was awake. I sat down and introduced myself to her as a minister of the Gospel. I then asked her what was wrong with her. It turned out that she was not drunk at all, as I had initially assumed, but was in great pain. She was incurably ill and had suffered for many years, being plagued with such excruciating pains that she could not even sit up straight or move her body.

I then asked her the first thing that next popped up in my mind, "Why are you sick?" An odd question indeed, but at times the Spirit of God does lead us to say and to do some strange things! Her reply was straight and immediate, "I am sick because I have sinned so much."

I was taken aback at her reply, but it made everything very easy because I could now tell her that she would not have to suffer any more. Jesus had borne all her sins and all her diseases; therefore her sins were forgiven, and so she would not have to suffer the painful consequences of sin any more!

I then told her how the Lord Jesus upon the cross had paid in full the price for all her sins and her diseases, and then asked her whether she wanted to receive the Him into her heart and give all her sins and diseases to Him. "Yes," she whispered through her pain. It was simple. I first prayed the sinners' prayer with her. I then rebuked the spirit of infirmity that was in her, and in the Name of Jesus Christ commanded it to be gone from her once and for all. For good measure, I pointed to the window of the train and told the devil to leave her, leave the train, and never come back again!

In an instant, the power of God came down all over her, and she was made whole.

She immediately jumped up from the berth where she lay and launched into some totally un-Swedish behavior, dancing, shouting, and praising God at the top of her voice. The ticket inspector came in precisely then. He opened the door and made the traditional announcement of railway ticket inspectors worldwide, "Tickets please!" The old lady looked at him and lunged forward towards him, waving her arms wildly and shouting, "Jesus has healed me! I am healed! I am healed!" The poor ticket inspector jumped backwards, his eyes almost popping out of their sockets. Frightened, he shut the door and ran off without checking our tickets.

The old lady then ran out of the coupe to the other compartments in the train and began to loudly testify to the other passengers of what the Lord had done for her. Needless to say, this created quite a stir amongst the passengers in the train, because Swedes are an extremely quiet and reserved people. This lady's extremely effervescent display of emotion was most unusual and exceedingly un-Swedish.

The interesting thing here is that I never encouraged her to do any of this. It was all her own reaction to what the Lord had done for her.

She then ran into the compartment where all the Lutheran priests were sitting and began to shout out what the Lord had done for her. Some of them rejoiced but others hid their faces in the newspapers and theological books that they were reading. This was because they were very upset at Ulf Ekman and at me. They were angry at us because we preached faith and also because of our clear-cut beliefs about the Baptism with the Holy Ghost. It was "most un-Lutheran," they said.

Another reason why they were so miserably unhappy with us was because they were "High Church," and in their belief system only those who were ordained through the laying on of hands of their Bishops in the historical line of "apostolic succession" could lay hands upon the sick. This had been a major point of contention that had been debated at the conference, but without any resolution. They were very upset at me because I was very bold in laying my hands upon and praying for the sick even though I did not fit into their doctrine of "apostolic succession." No bishop had ever laid his hands upon me, so how could God ever use me? Ulf Ekman, as my immediate senior, supported me fully. Never having much tolerance for religious nonsense, I did not really care much for what they thought, and did just as I felt led to do by the Lord. This, of course, did not sit well with them and only added to further stoke their anger towards me.

And now, this miracle had taken place and torpedoed this aspect of their theology that was so extremely important to them. Should they rejoice that God had used someone who was not ordained by their bishops? Should they get angry at me once more?

They decided to quietly swallow their pride and say nothing.

A couple weeks after this incident, I received a phone call from the South of Sweden. It was a Miss Ulla Johansson, a very well-known and respected former missionary who had heard about the miracle on the train from some of the Lutheran priests who were present when it had happened. I knew Ulla quite well, and after exchanging some pleasantries she asked me whether I would be willing to go and minister in her old home church, a small Lutheran church in the town of Angelholm in Southern Sweden. I felt most honored that she would ask me to do this, and I accepted.

I took the train down to Angelholm to minister over a weekend, from Friday to Sunday. This was the summer of 1981. On the first evening, only around 50 people came out to listen to this unknown young preacher. The Spirit of God moved mightily and around 40 of the 50 people present were baptized with the Holy Ghost and with Fire. The pastor was knocked out under the power of God and began to speak in other tongues. He could not stop, but spoke in tongues incessantly from that moment all through the night, until the next day. His wife, rather alarmed, told me the next day that he had not slept a wink that night but had been up until late in the morning speaking in tongues and worshiping God.

On the second evening, God touched many people and there were wonderful manifestations of different kinds of healings and miracles. By then, word began to spread about the things that the Lord was doing in these meetings.

Twenty miles away from Angelholm is the coastal city of Helsingborg. There lived a well-to-do couple with their three children, a girl and two boys. The youngest child, a boy called Matthias, suffered from an incurable bone disease that

31

had left him unable to use his legs or walk. I was told that he was the third known case in the world with this unusual disease; it was so rare that they did not even have a name for it. The disease was draining all the calcium from his bones and making them brittle like matchsticks. The family had taken the boy to top specialists in several different countries looking for a cure. They had spent a lot of money doing this, but it was to no avail. Medical researchers and physicians in several countries were working on his case and trying to create a medicine for him but had not found a cure yet. In the meantime, his body was crippled and wasting away.

Somebody told the boy's mother about the meetings and she came to the little church for the final service on Sunday night. I remember her very well as she sat in the last row with her crippled son on her lap. I remember her listening intently, watching my every move as I preached. When I called people to come to the front for prayer she was the first one to rise from her seat to come forward. Before I prayed for her crippled son, I first asked her whether she had any sin in her life. I normally do not do this, but in this particular case I felt led by the Holy Spirit to do so. She began to cry and told me that she had been a Christian earlier in her youth and had served the Lord; but then she had met and fallen in love with an unbeliever. She had married him (her present husband) and because they did not share any spiritual values together, she had over time stopped going to church. She just "drifted away" from her faith in Jesus and was now very far from God. She lived more or less like a regular heathen person.

I asked her to turn back to Jesus and to ask Him for forgiveness for her sins. She closed her eyes and asked God for forgiveness, with her tears washing her mascara down her face. Once that was done, I said to her, "Your sins are now forgiven; your relationship with Jesus is restored. Now there is nothing that can stop you from receiving a miracle from God!"

I then anointed the little boy with oil in the mighty Name of our Lord Jesus. Laying my hands upon his head, I prayed the prayer of faith, asking God to heal him. I then stepped back and looked at him. There was no visible change in his outward condition, and he still looked just as crippled as he did before; but I knew that because the Word of God is always true, Jesus had touched him and God's healing power was at work in his body even as we looked at him.

The woman then asked me, "What should I do now?"

I said to her, "You don't have to do anything. God has done it. Just thank God daily that your son is healed. Every time you look at him, thank God that Jesus bore his diseases upon His own self, and that because He suffered, your son has been healed!"

I said this because the Bible says:

> *"For verily I say unto you, That whosoever shall say unto this mountain, Be thou removed, and be thou cast into the sea; and shall not doubt in his heart, but shall believe that those things which he saith shall come to pass; he shall have whatsoever he saith. Therefore I say unto you, What things soever ye desire, when ye pray, believe that ye receive them, and ye shall have them."* Mark 11:23-24

"Believe that ye receive them, and ye shall have them." It simply means that the "believing" comes before the "having." In the world it is "seeing is believing," but in God's realm of faith it is the other way around. It is "believing is seeing." If we believe that we have received it even before we physically have it, then we shall have it!

Faith is to have an assurance that God has heard our prayer and that He has already answered and given us what we have asked for, even before we physically see the answer before our eyes.

Faith is to claim possession of something that God in His Word has declared to be ours. Faith boldly proclaims one's possession of it and boldly declares "I have it!" even before one actually sees it manifested physically. I like to put it this way, *"If you got it, you'll get it!"*

The Bible declares that our God is, *"God that gives life to the dead and calls those things that be not as though they were"* (Romans 4:17)!

In other words, God speaks about things that do not yet exist in the physical as though they already exist. That is what I call "The God kind of talk." As God's children, we should speak the same way. Declaring the existence of things even before they exist in the natural is the "the language of faith." This is how Jesus spoke after Lazarus had died. Everybody knew that Lazarus was dead, but Jesus said,

> *"Our friend Lazarus sleepeth; but I go, that I may awake him out of sleep."* John 11:11

Lazarus was dead, but Jesus spoke not the obvious but what He saw through the "eyes of faith." Jesus spoke His faith rather than that which the physical eyes could see in the natural. This is what faith is.

Then again, we see Jesus do the same thing before He raised Jairus's daughter from the dead. Everybody knew that the little girl was dead, but Jesus said,

> *"The damsel is not dead, but sleepeth."* Mark 5:39

Once again, we see Jesus speaking not the obvious but that

which He saw through the eyes of faith!

To live a miracle-filled life we must learn to talk "the God kind of talk." Otherwise, we will be reduced to only believing and speaking out that which our physical eyes can see, which is NOT faith. Faith sees beyond the natural. Faith sees the unseen, embraces it, possesses it, confesses it, and loudly affirms it.

Seeing what God sees and talking like God talks. That is the essence of what faith is, pure and simple.

> *"And this is the confidence that we have in him, that, if we ask any thing according to his will, he heareth us: And if we know that he hear us, whatsoever we ask, we know that we have the petitions that we desired of him."*
> 1 John 5:14-15

For a man or woman of faith, it is not "seeing is believing," but rather "believing is seeing." If you believe that you have it, it is yours!

But, what is it that gives us the right to proclaim that we possess something that is not yet visible to the eye nor manifested in the natural? The Word of God, of course! Anything that God has declared in the Bible as belonging to us is ours because of the writ of Almighty God. We can therefore take hold of it by faith, by believing and proclaiming that we have it; that it is ours. Even if we do not see it or feel it in the natural, it is ours because God says so. This is how we receive and possess salvation, righteousness, healing, and every other blessing that belongs to every child of God.

The lady said that she would do as I had asked her to, that she would continuously thank God that her son was healed no matter what she saw with her eyes. I thanked God that she was not brainwashed by religious unbelief. Religious people are the hardest people to minister healing to; because even though they may be sincere, their minds are loaded with a mixture of pious-sounding religious theories and pure unbelief that have been taught to them by eloquent preachers who have mastered the art of covering up their own unbelief with impressive intellectual discourses. As Rev. Charles Price, one of my British teachers in Bible School, used to say, tongue-in-cheek and with a twinkle in his eye, "Blessed are they that expect nothing, for they shall not be disappointed."

This woman was not like that. She desperately wanted a miracle and was ready to take hold of what God had promised in His Word, no matter what the cost.

I took the train back home to Uppsala the next morning. All through the 7 hour journey, my mind was continually bombarded with thoughts such as, "You have made a huge fool of yourself!" and "You prayed for the boy and nothing happened. Then you told the boy's mother to thank God that her son has been healed; although everybody could see that the boy was not healed."

For hours, I fought and resisted these thoughts, speaking the Word of God to counter them. I knew that these thoughts were from Satan and I knew what Satan was trying to do; he was trying to get me to let go of faith and lean on human logic instead. He wanted me to believe that which I saw with my eyes instead of that which God has spoken in His Word. This ploy of Satan is one of the Christian's worst enemies. Yielding to it would "abort" the miracle that God was doing in that little boy's body, because unbelief has the capability to destroy a miracle faster than anything else. I knew that if I yielded to Satan's logic and agreed with him instead of holding fast to and believing God's Word, the battle would be lost.

God gave me strength and I held on tenaciously, speaking the Word of God and praying in tongues. I rebuked the devil again and again and kept on proclaiming that the Word of God is true and that God has done it; that what He has promised He is also mighty to perform. I believed that I had prayed according to the Word of God and that because God's Word is true, it was done!

In times like this, mere mental assent with the Word of God is not enough. One must speak the Word out aggressively, get vocal about it, and proclaim it. The battle in my mind was so intense that I had to speak it out loudly to hold on to the victory that Christ had won, so I went to a few of my fellow passengers on the train and told them about the little boy's healing. Most Swedes are very heathen and godless, and these people looked at me as if I was a nutcase. Actually, it would be more accurate to say that some of them were totally frightened out of their wits. One old gentleman even asked me whether I belonged to one of those "tongue-talking brainwashed Zionist cults!" I finally found a Pentecostal missionary on the train. When I told him the story, he began to rejoice with me and we praised the Lord and prayed together. I clearly remember how we sang the old Pentecostal song,

> *"Filled with God, yes, Filled with God,*
> *Pardoned and cleansed and filled with God,*
> *Filled with God, yes, Filled with God,*
> *Emptied of self, and Filled with God"*

Upon arriving home, I received a phone call from the pastor in Angelholm. He was breathless with excitement. He told me that the mother of the lame boy had called to tell him that her son had suddenly gotten up, walked one step and then fallen down again. The pastor then gave me the lady's telephone number and asked me to call her. I called the lady immediately, and she told me what had happened. "What should I do?" she asked me. "Just keep on thanking God that your son has been healed," I replied.

The lady called me the next day, very excited. "Brother Christopher!" she said. "My son stood up today, walked four steps and then fell down again! What should I do?" "Just keep on thanking God that your son has been healed!" I replied.

She called me again the third day. "Brother Christopher!" she exclaimed. "He stood up today and walked all the way across the living room, but then he fell down again. What do you want me to do?" "Just keep on thanking God that your son has been healed!" I replied.

Then came the fourth day, the phone rang. It was the lady. She was laughing, crying, and totally hysterical with joy. "Brother Christopher!" she screamed into the receiver. "My son stood up this morning and has been walking, running, jumping, and playing all day! He is perfectly well! I am so thankful to Jesus for everything that He has done!"

To God be all the Glory! We both rejoiced and glorified God for what He had done.

I saw the boy again some years later. He was still walking and running, perfectly healthy and well. I spoke to his mother recently and found out that he is now an expert carpenter who travels and works all over the world.

With our God nothing is impossible!

It is important to notice that in this case the total manifestation of healing did not come instantly; it took four days. Sometimes it can take longer, sometimes shorter. I have seen many people receive instant manifestations of healing, but then I have seen others who have had to wait a long time. I remember a paraplegic boy who was brought to one of our meetings in Gorzow Wielkepolska in Poland. After I prayed for him, his family asked me the same question that the mother of the little boy in Sweden had asked, "What do we do now?" I gave them the same answer, "Just keep on thanking God that your son has been healed!" It took a year of slow and gradual improvement, but by the end of the year the boy was totally healed.

Why is it that at times God heals people instantly, but then at other times He chooses to take time in doing so? This is a good question, the answer to which nobody but the Lord alone knows. I always say that this is one of the questions I shall ask the Lord when we finally see Him in Heaven; but then, when we reach that City of Glory, when we finally see Him face to Face and behold Him in all His Glory, all such questions shall fade away into irrelevancy!

So, although God chooses not to reveal all things to us whilst we are in this world, He does, through His Word and by His Spirit, reveal everything that we need to know in this life in order to follow Jesus and to walk in victory over Satan, sin, death, and disease. Now we see through a glass, darkly, but there will come that glorious morning when we shall see and understand all things. The Bible says:

"The secret things belong to the LORD our God, but the things revealed belong to us and to our sons forever."
Deuteronomy 29:29

Christianity came from the East. I am an Easterner, and for us Christianity is to be lived out of the heart; with love, with passion, and with faith. One of the biggest drawbacks of the Western mind is that the Westerner, being more intellectual and educated than the Easterner, lives Christianity more out of his head than his heart. Everything has to make sense and be understood logically; otherwise it becomes very difficult for him to "believe." He finds it hard to believe unless his mind can make sense of it. The western man then builds a "theology" consisting solely of the things that make sense to him intellectually, a "mental" kind of Christianity.

The important thing is not to have the ability to understand God logically, but to first know Him and the goodness of His nature as revealed in His Word. Then to trust in His Word, knowing that He is always good in all things and that His Word is always unfailing and true.

Always remember that God loved us so much that He gave His only begotten Son to die for us upon the cross, taking upon Himself all our sins, all our diseases, all our torments, and all our poverty. Knowing this, we should live our lives with joy, always full of faith, and daily expecting miracles and good things from God.

> *"Blessed be the Lord, who daily loadeth us with benefits, even the God of our salvation."* Psalm 68:19

So great is the love of God that He is always for us, and He is more eager to bless us, heal us, and touch us than we could ever understand!

Knowing THAT is the foundation on which a life of solid and victorious faith stands!

We held a crusade in Chegutu, Zimbabwe in July of 2007. On the last night, I spoke out the Word of Knowledge that the Lord would heal a child with a deformed leg.

A man came forward carrying his 6 month old son wrapped in a blanket. I saw that the boy's one leg was twisted and paralyzed and the foot was a club foot, twisted with the sole pointing upward. I prayed for the little foot. After prayer, the foot still looked the same. I said to the father, "It is all right now. The foot is well." He looked down, first at the foot that still looked as deformed as before, then at me. He looked at me incredulously and said, "Is it really healed?"

I said, "Go home, the foot is all right."

You see, this was not "mind over matter," neither was I "confessing to make something happen." I was merely talking "the God kind of talk." We had done our part, and God would complete His part when we lined up our talk with His Word.

A few days later, the man showed up at our next crusade in Kadoma, another town about 20 miles away. He was smiling from ear to ear. "Pastor!" he exclaimed. "My son is healed! His leg is healed! His foot is straight!" He brought the baby the next day for everybody to see. The foot and leg were perfect.

You see, I could have "aborted" the miracle by not being in agreement with God's Word and saying, "Oh, I guess nothing has happened. Your son is not healed…" Had I said that, we would have missed out on this wonderful miracle that God was doing. That is why it is always best to agree with and to say what God says in His Word, to talk the God kind of talk, no matter what we feel or what we see.

Making "talking the God kind of talk" a way of life and aligning our thoughts and words with the Word of God causes us to live our lives in a never-ending flow of God's miracle power!

Chapter 5

THE LITTLE GIRL
PILA, POLAND

Pila is a town a few hours drive away east of the city of Poznan, in Northern Poland. There is a huge cathedral-like Roman Catholic church in the city. The senior priest of that church at that time, a very kind old gentleman, was very hungry for the power of God. He had thrown open the doors of his church to me to come to minister to his congregation. He and I had become good friends. I would go to Poland every summer with a large team of students from the Bible school in Sweden where I was a teacher. During these trips, I would always go to Pila to hold a service in my friend's church.

It was a warm July evening and thousands of people had packed the church for the service, their hearts full of great expectation of what God would do. There were people everywhere; on the platform, behind the altar, in the vestry, and packed into every nook and cranny of the huge old church. The place was full, packed solid to the brim; I had a few feet of space in front of the altar where I could stand, move, and minister.

I have always enjoyed ministering to Roman Catholics. They have a depth of reverence for the person of the Lord

Jesus, for His Cross, and for His Blood that touches my heart. They also respond with great faith for healings and miracles. In fact, some of the most outstanding miracles that I have ever seen have been in services in Roman Catholic churches.

The presence of God was mighty and tangible that evening. We worshiped God. I preached a simple gospel message and thousands responded to the altar call for salvation. The Holy Spirit was present and the very air seemed to vibrate with the presence of God. The atmosphere was indescribable. I felt God's Holy presence with every breath I took.

I then began to pray for the people, calling upon the mighty name of the Lord Jesus. I sensed that the Spirit of God was moving over the people. Miracles began to happen all throughout the crowd. Catholic churches are not noisy places like our Pentecostal churches. Here and there one could hear someone whimper and others breaking into sobs, otherwise it was mostly quiet. Then suddenly, there was a loud noise behind me. Somebody screamed. I turned to look. People began to weep, scream, and cry out. I looked towards the source of the commotion, at the hundreds of people who were seated behind the altar. By then, they were weeping and screaming hysterically. I looked at my team of Swedes and Norwegians from the Bible school, who were also seated behind the altar. They too were crying, and with tears streaming down their cheeks they were shouting at me in Swedish and Norwegian. They were pointing to something on their side of the altar across from me. I looked in that direction and could see the top of a little blond head moving forward. I walked over around the altar and saw that it was a little girl about nine years old. From the way she walked I understood immediately that she had been paralyzed and was now walking for the first time in her life.

Let me interrupt this account by telling the story of this little girl. She was around nine years of age, the daughter of a family from that parish. The priest knew them very well because they never missed a Mass. The little girl had been born paralyzed and deformed, with her body locked in a fetal position. Her mouth was perpetually open, with a steady dribble of saliva constantly flowing down her chin. Her arms, hands, fingers, wrists, legs, and feet were bent and deformed. Her knees were drawn up to her chin and her heels were drawn up to her buttocks. Her legs seemed to have no muscles. Not one part of her was what one would call "normal" or straight. She was totally twisted, paralyzed and had never stood on her legs before. Her mother had brought her to the service and sat behind the altar holding her crippled little daughter upon her lap.

The presence of our God and Savior was so indescribably mighty in that place that night. The people stood in awe as I preached the old story of the Cross, the death and the resurrection of our Lord Jesus. At the same time, God was doing something indescribable in the heart of that mother. She was gripped by the holy presence of Jesus and by the Spirit of faith that always accompanies His presence. It is impossible for man to describe the workings of God in the depths of a person's heart and soul, therefore I cannot really say much about how exactly God moved in that mother's heart that evening; but, in what I can only describe as a sheer impulse of faith she suddenly put her paralyzed daughter down on the floor. As soon as she did so, the little girl's twisted and paralyzed limbs began to straighten out.

The people watching this behind the altar could hear the sounds of her bones and joints cracking as God began to straighten her out and heal her by His mighty power. The power of He who created the universe by His Hand was touching her; His life-giving healing power coursed through

45

her body, making her whole. The people watched in awe and amazement. Then the little girl, with her newfound strength, began to rise up from the floor whereon she lay. She arose, stood upright on her legs, and slowly began to walk. The people began to scream, shout, and weep. The little girl then began to walk around the altar towards where I was standing.

I walked around the altar and saw the girl. I understood immediately that God had done a miracle and healed this child. I took her by the hand and we began to walk together towards the front of the altar. I had taken a few steps when the immensity of what God had done struck me. I was suddenly afraid lest anyone look at me or my faith as the cause of this miracle. It was all Jesus, and I did not have anything to do with it. I remember falling down on my knees and shouting in the microphone, "I have nothing to do with this! This is not the ministry of a man; this is the ministry of Jesus!"

I felt so unworthy and small before the mighty and holy presence of Jesus that filled that place; in my nothingness, I began to weep, looking for a place where I could hide. I crawled down under the altar, curled up in a corner, and wept like a child. I had just seen and touched the glory and power of the Lord Jesus. I felt like the prophet Isaiah when he was in the presence of God and could only cry out, *"Woe is me for I am undone..."* (Isaiah 6:5)! At that moment, I really believed that I would die. Surely no man could see so much of the glory of God and live; and I had seen the glory of the Lord! I believed that at that moment God would take me home. I wept in my own unworthiness before the holy presence of God and began to pray, asking Him to take care of Britta and our little children once I was gone...

Then, I suddenly heard the voice of the Lord. It was

unmistakably clear and shook me. He said, "Get up and go stand before the people and minister to them. You have not seen anything as yet!" I was shaken. I crawled out from under the altar and looked, and this is the scene that met my eyes; I saw six boys of varying ages, all crippled, being carried by their parents to the front. I saw their parents put them up on the platform and as soon as their feet touched the platform they all stood up and began to walk. No one had prayed for them, nor did anyone ever touch them. It was Jesus and Jesus alone. Miracles were happening all over the place.

I stood up. The crowd of thousands began to push to get to the front. The packed mass of humanity was surging forward, and I was being pushed up against the concrete altar; if I did not do something quickly I could be crushed against the altar. These disciplined, serious, and normally quiet Polish Catholic people were getting out of control. I then took off my jacket and threw it into the crowd shouting, "The anointing of God is in my jacket. Anybody who touches it will be healed!"

I stood and watched my jacket being passed around the crowd. I saw thousands of people touch my jacket. Many clutched it as a token of faith to their chests, weeping and calling out to Jesus. The awesome presence of Jesus still filled that place. My team and I stayed there late into the night ministering to the people.

I went back to Pila the next year, and the parish priest told me something most amazing. He said that for three months after the previous year's service a line of people would be at the door of his parsonage every single day to testify of many wonderful miracles that the Lord had continued to do after that service. People brought wheelchairs, crutches, spectacles, back braces, neck braces, hearing aids, artificial limbs, doctors' reports, etc and told of the wonderful miracles that the Lord had done for them.

The power of the Holy Spirit is mighty beyond human comprehension. God can do far above that which we can even imagine or ask. This is the wonderful thing about the Christian life. We serve the living God, who not only meets the needs of those who reach out to Him, but He does far above and beyond that which the human mind has the capacity to grasp!

> *"Now unto him that is able to do exceeding abundantly above all that we ask or think, according to the power that worketh in us, Unto him be glory in the church by Christ Jesus throughout all ages, world without end. Amen."*
> Ephesians 3:20-21

Chapter 6

THE YOUNG WOMAN
WITH THE DEFORMED JAW

WARSZAWA, POLAND

This wonderful miracle took place in one of my visits to Warsaw, Poland. I often used to minister in one of the largest and most well-known churches in that city, a huge cathedral-like building with four tall spires rising high into the sky. The parish priest was very open and welcoming, and God did great and wonderful things every time I had the opportunity to minister there. I basically had an open door there any time I wanted to come. They would never advertise, but even if I gave them a week's notice they would spread the news by word-of-mouth and thousands of eager and hungry souls would come and pack the building out to hear the Word of God.

It was a summer evening in 1988, and I had a team with me from the Bible school in Sweden where I used to teach. We had traveled around and ministered all over Poland for three weeks. We had many fruitful meetings all over the country and were now headed back home to Sweden. We drove to Warsaw where we would hold our last meeting of that particular trip. From Warsaw, we would drive on to Gdansk to catch the 18 hour long ferry to Nynashamn in Sweden. A further three hour drive from Nynashamn would see us safely back home in Uppsala.

We drove to the big church in Warsaw. As always, the building was packed with thousands of people. Every available inch of space was taken by the sea of humanity that had managed to wedge itself inside the building. Hundreds stood outside because there was not even standing room for them inside. I preached that night from Psalm 103:1-3, *"Bless the LORD, O my soul: and all that is within me, bless his holy name. Bless the LORD, O my soul, and forget not all his benefits: Who forgiveth all thine iniquities; who healeth all thy diseases."*

At the end of my message, I gave the altar call for people to receive Jesus Christ as their Lord and Savior. A large multitude of souls responded. After leading them in a prayer to receive Jesus, I began to pray a mass prayer for the sick. The power of the Lord began to move over the people, and God began to do miracles all over the place.

In the rear part of the sanctuary, in that great multitude of people, stood a young lady born with a terrible facial deformity. Her entire jaw bone was severely deformed making her face look terribly twisted and grotesque. She was lonely and had very few friends, having grown up all through her childhood being mercilessly teased and taunted because of her physical appearance. When she had reached her late teens, she had sought medical help. Some kind surgeons had taken her plight to heart and had begun to work on her face with reconstructive surgery. They had cut her jawbone and other bones in her skull in different places, and were rebuilding and reconstructing the bone structure. The pieces were then rejoined and held together with metal screws, pins, and plates. Whenever she would touch her face she could actually feel the plates and screws under her skin.

They had told her that it was going to be a long and tedious process that would take years of reconstructive surgery.

She had come to this meeting after having heard from people how Jesus could work miracles and heal the sick, and now she stood in the rear part of the crowd waiting for Jesus to touch her. I began to pray and what happened next can only be best described in her own words:

"I closed my eyes when you began to pray, and suddenly I felt the wonderful presence of God envelop my entire being. I then felt the warm hands of God on my face, on my jaw. I dared not open my eyes because I knew that it was Jesus. It was such a warm and Holy feeling. The hands of God were on both sides of my face. I felt the warmth of His hands for about a minute, as they moved on my face, and then those gentle and warm hands were lifted away. When you stopped praying I opened my eyes. I was in a daze; I put my hands up to my face and was amazed because for the first time in my life I could feel that my face was perfectly symmetrical and whole. The metal plates, pins and screws that held the pieces of my jaw bone together were gone. Hitherto I could feel them every time I touched my face, but now they were gone. Those who knew me and stood around me turned and looked at me. Some began to scream. Others began to cry. They reached out to touch my face, looked at me and wept and hugged me. Look at me now! I was so ugly, that nobody would even look at me, but see, look at what Jesus has done for me!"

When this young lady finally came up to the platform to testify of what the Lord had done, many of the people in the crowd who knew her first gasped in wonderment. Then, some began to shout, to weep, and to praise God. I looked at her. She was beautiful, or as one would say, "drop dead gorgeous," like a movie star or a model. It was hard

51

for me to fathom that such a beautiful young woman had been so deformed, too grotesque to look at. I thought of the scripture:

> *"To give unto them beauty for ashes, the oil of joy for mourning, the garment of praise for the spirit of heaviness; that they might be called trees of righteousness, the planting of the LORD, that he might be glorified."* Isaiah 61:3

Chapter 7

HE AIN'T HEAVY, HE'S MY BROTHER
LUSAKA, ZAMBIA

It was March 2005. We were holding a crusade in one of the townships that surrounds the city of Lusaka the capital of Zambia. Huge multitudes were coming to the crusade every night to hear the Gospel. People were receiving Jesus Christ into their lives and God was working many wonderful and powerful miracles of healing and deliverance. God was doing a great work among the people of that town.

There lived a family a little over a mile away from the field where we were holding our crusade. The husband and wife had absolutely no interest in the Gospel; believing that all preachers were interested in nothing else but people's money. They would spend most of their evenings at a nearby bar, leaving their children behind at home. There were two children in the family, a girl of 11 and her younger brother who was only nine years old. The little boy was born normal, but had contracted a deadly form of meningitis as a little baby. The disease had left him paralyzed and he had never been able to stand or to walk since then. As a result he would be in bed all day. When his parents go to the bar in the evenings, they would tell his sister to look after him.

53

Now we have a large PA system that we use in our Africa crusades, and under good conditions our preaching, singing and testimonies can be heard a couple of miles away. This way we can reach out to a large area around us and ensure that as many people as possible hear the Gospel of our Lord Jesus.

Huge multitudes of people came out to the field to attend the crusade on the first two nights. The crusade was the talk of the town, but this family never came. The parents, as usual, would go out to the bar to drink with their friends, telling their 11-year-old daughter to look after her little brother. They did not have a television in the house, but through the open window of the bedroom the paralyzed little boy could hear the preaching of the Gospel from over a mile away. Our large PA system was carrying the Gospel message of life and hope in Jesus all the way into his bedroom. The little boy listened intently to the Gospel message and then to the testimonies of people who were being healed.

The third evening came. The parents, as their habit was, went out to the bar and asked their daughter to look after her little brother. As soon as the parents had left the little boy turned to his sister and begged her, "Could you please carry me to where that preacher is preaching about Jesus? I know that if you carry me there His Jesus going to heal me!"

Their 11-year-old girl looked at her little brother, and said, "You are almost as big as me. You are heavy, how can I carry you so far?"

"Please try, this is my only chance. I want to walk again. If you carry me there, I know his Jesus will heal me!" he pleaded, "Please, I promise that you won't have to carry me back; Jesus will heal me and I shall walk back home on my own legs!"

His sister then decided that she would do her best for her little brother. "Okay, you are heavy, but I shall try!" she said.

With great difficulty she put her little brother who was almost as big as her, up on her back. She then began to walk towards the general direction of where the sound of the crusade was coming from. It was a long walk carrying that heavy burden of love; she fell down several times on the way, but each time she fell she would get up and pick up her little brother once again upon her back and continue walking towards the crusade. She knew that this was his only chance. They had been to hospitals, they had been to witchdoctors but there was no help for brother. Only Jesus could do it. Their parents were not there for them, but they, although they were mere small children, they had faith in Jesus. Her little brother's faith was stronger than hers because he somehow seemed to KNOW that he would be healed. He just knew it and that is why he had been so insistent when he had asked her to carry him to the crusade.

The long walk of love, the walk of faith from their home to the crusade ground was painful. By the time they finally arrived in the crusade her elbows and knees were skinned and bleeding from all the times that she had fallen walking to the crusade with the burden of love upon her back. There Jesus looked at the little boy's faith, touched him and healed him. He arose and began to walk, haltingly at first and the more confidently. He begin to run, the crowd began to shout and rejoice. He then came up to the platform hand-in-hand with his big sister. Healed, triumphant, although somewhat dazed because he was standing on his legs and walking for the first time in his life.

It was a most wonderful sight to behold!

They went back walking home hand in hand from the crusade. They arrived home and stayed up until their parents came. The parents were taken by amazement when they saw their paralyzed little son walking. The rejoiced and wept. The next night they were all back in the crusade. The whole family received Jesus Christ as their Lord and Savior and received God's ultimate miracle; the gift of eternal life through our Lord Jesus Christ.

God is a good God. He honors even the faith of little children. The Bible says, *"And Jesus called a little child unto him, and set him in the midst of them, and said, Verily I say unto you, Except ye be converted, and become as little children, ye shall not enter into the kingdom of heaven. Whosoever therefore shall humble himself as this little child, the same is greatest in the kingdom of heaven"* (Matthew 18:2-3).

We lived in the world where education and intellect are valued highly. But the thing that God values far above education or intellect is faith. Some have such highly developed intellects that faith can often be a difficult thing for them. For children it is not so; they are still simple, pliable, trusting. In their simplicity they find it easy to believe God and to trust God for miracles.

God is not asking us to despise education or intelligence; all he asks of us is to humble ourselves and to become trusting and believing as little children. That is how we receive salvation and enter into the kingdom of heaven. Children have not yet learnt to develop negative qualities such as skepticism, unbelief and cynicism; but respond with faith and trust. That is also precisely how we partake of miracles, healings, the blessing and provisions of God's Kingdom, and all the other wonderful things that God has promised to us through His Son Jesus Christ!

> *"Verily I say unto you, Whosoever shall not receive the kingdom of God as a little child shall in no wise enter therein."* Luke 18:17

PHOTOS

From the stories in this book

Chapter 3
The paralyzed man from Bialka, Poland with his wife one year after his healing.

Chapter 11
The crippled Hindu RSS leader at the time he was healed.

Chapter 13
Graciela 10
years after her
deliverance,
with Christopher,
her mother, and
her aunt.

Chapter 14
The little lame boy
after the meeting in
which he was healed

Chapter 16
Immanuel
with the deaf
mute man,
immediately
after he was
healed.

PHOTOS

Other miracles from throughout the years

Bulgaria, 1991
With a team
member after a
service

Zambia, 1999
A lame man walks
with Christopher

Zambia, 1996
A lame man walks

Zimbabwe, 1994
She was totally paralyzed, but now pushes the wheelbarrow in which she was brought to the meeting

Rosario, Argentina
1996

Tanzania, 1998
A girl, who was paralyzed, jumps and dances after being healed

Burma, 1997
A deaf-mute girl healed

Zambia, 1997
She was paralyzed and was carried to the crusade in this wheelbarrow

Zimbabwe, 1997
A blind man
receives his sight

Burma, 2000
Lame lady, who was healed,
holding her crutches

Argentina, 1998
Woman's arm was
paralyzed and stuck

Burma, 1998
A deaf lady receives
her healing

Zambia, 1999
Blind and paralyzed
man healed

Zimbabwe, 2007
Woman, who was
paralyzed and deaf as a
result of a stroke, is healed
and now dances for joy

Chapter 8

THE CRIPPLED POLICE OFFICER

MKOBA, ZIMBABWE

I was holding a crusade in the township of Mkoba, just outside the city of Gweru in Zimbabwe. The crusade stirred up the whole town and tens of thousands of people were coming out to hear the Word of God. The meetings were held in a large open field right in the middle of Mkoba. Across the field opposite our platform from which I was preaching, there were a number of "beer halls" filled with drunks. Many of these drunks would come to the crusade every evening to loudly mock what was happening.

One night after I had preached and done the altar call for people to receive Christ, I invited the sick to the front of the crowd for prayer. This night an extraordinarily large number of sick, crippled paralyzed and infirm people were brought to the front. The first to come was a woman pushing a wheelbarrow. I was watching her as she came all the way to the front and parked the wheelbarrow directly in front of me. I was on an eight-foot high platform and from my vantage point I looked down into the wheelbarrow.

What I saw at first looked like a bundle of rags; and then I was shocked to realize that there was actually a person lying in the wheelbarrow. It was a fully grown man who appeared to have shrunken down to almost nothing. His arms and legs, paralyzed and emaciated, hung down from the sides of the wheelbarrow. His eyes were sunken deep into their sockets and were totally devoid of any expression. I later found out that this man was paralyzed and was dying and that the woman who had pushed the wheelbarrow to the crusade was his wife. She had heard about the wonderful things that the Lord Jesus was doing in the crusade. Her heart had been field with faith and with expectation, and she had walked a long way to the crusade pushing her paralyzed and dying husband in that wheelbarrow.

Many other people surrounded her, some were carried there paralyzed. Some were were crippled and on crutches. Others were blind and were led there by relatives, whilst others were deaf. My heart was overwhelmed as I saw the vast number of diseased and infirm people who so desperately needed a touch from Jesus. I began to pray for the sick; and the Lord suddenly spoke to me. I heard Him say, "There is a man in the crowd who is crippled and on crutches. I am healing him right now!"

I thought, "Lord, there are so many people here who are paralyzed, crippled, and on crutches..."

But then there is this one thing that I have learnt in life. It is always best to obey God without letting our minds get in the way! The Lord always knows what he is doing!

So I called out, "The Lord is telling me that there is a man here, crippled and on crutches, Jesus is healing you right now. Drop your right crutches now and run!"

I suddenly saw a movement in one side of the crowd. Something stirred, and I looked and saw a man throw his crutches up into the air and begin to run. People began to shout. Some began to run after him. The whole crowd seemed to go totally wild. People were shouting, jumping up and down praising God whilst this man ran all over the place. He was very visible because he was dressed in white, wearing a white shirt and white trousers.

This account would not be complete if I did not write a little bit here about the background story of this man.

This man was one of Zimbabwe's first motorcycle police officers. When the police force in Zimbabwe first acquired motorcycles and the first motorcycle officers went on patrol, it was a matter of great pride for the nation. The names and the pictures of these officers were in the newspapers. This man, a local son of Mkoba, was one of them. The whole community was very proud of him. Soon after this he was involved in a serious accident when his motorcycle went off the road at high speed and turned around many times leaving him severely injured. Both his legs were crushed and broken. I was told that the bones in his legs and hips were crushed into very small pieces. He was left crippled and had been invalidated out of the service. The story of this unfortunate accident had been in the news and everybody in town knew of what had happened to him.

He had hobbled to the crusade on his crutches, and then Jesus had touched him. He heard the words, "there is a man here, crippled and on crutches, Jesus is healing you right now. Drop your crutches now and run!" He felt the power of Jesus Christ stirring, moving and then surging through body. He felt his broken bones coming together. It electrified him. Jesus was there!

That was it. He threw his crutches into the air and began to run as fast as he could, shouting and praising God. All the people there had also heard the word that came forth, and seen him throw the crutches away, and began to run. They recognized him and saw that this was a genuine miracle performed by God. They too now begin to shout and praise God.

This miracle generated a powerful spirit of faith that went like a shock-wave of Holy Ghost power through the vast multitude. The view from the platform was amazing to behold; people were shouting, the huge crowd was out of control and beside themselves with joy. Looking down from the platform I saw the sick people who stood around the paralyzed and dying man in the wheelbarrow shouting at him, "Get up man! In the Name of Jesus get up! Jesus is here just like the preacher said! Get up from the wheelbarrow and run!"

I had never seen anything like it. The people were in the grip of the Spirit of Faith. Faith was everywhere; one could feel it, touch it. As they were shouting at the man in the wheelbarrow to get up, he began to stir. He began to move, slowly at first, he then sat up, somebody grabbed his arm and pulled him up. The man stood up and began to walk slowly, stumbling, the people around him shouting and cheering him on. Then he began to walk faster, even faster; then he was running... what a sight.... His hands were up in the air and he was running! The crowd was shouting and praising God; by then other people were dropping their crutches, coming out of the wheelbarrows they had been carried in, out of their wheelchairs, walking, jumping, and praising God. Miracles were happening all over the field.

Jesus of Nazareth had for a few moments stepped down from his Throne of Glory in Heaven and was walking through the crowd gathered on a dusty field in a poor town in Zimbabwe; people were being healed and everybody was seeing and experiencing the wonderful works of God.

Than I saw many drunks from the beer halls out across on the other side of the field come running to the front, get down on their knees in the dirt, repenting and asking Jesus to save them from their sins. I was told later that the power of God had sobered these men instantly as they knelt before Him in repentance!

One second, one touch of Jesus is more powerful than a hundred years of human effort. With God nothing is impossible. God is a miracle working God, and one miracle can unleash and flood of other miracles, touching many lives, healing many people, saving multitudes of sinners. This so that sinners may find the Savior and that Jesus the Son of God may be glorified!

Chapter 9

THE PARALYZED WOMAN
IN REV SZYMYNSKI'S CHURCH

POZNAN, POLAND

I was ministering in a Roman Catholic church in Poznan, Poland. The parish priest, Rev. Szymynski, and I had become friends during my first trip to Poland. Since then, I had a standing invitation to minister in his church any time that I wanted to. Because of this, I always made a stop in Poznan to minister at this church every time I went to Poland.

Large crowds of people used to come to these meetings expecting miracles from God. Even communists and atheists would come with great needs in their lives; for many of them this was their first ever visit to any kind of church. I would preach simple gospel messages about the crucified and the resurrected Jesus. This would release faith in the hearts of the people, and the Lord would then move in their hearts. Almost every person present who had not received Jesus Christ as their Lord and Savior would open their hearts to receive Him. After that, I would pray for the sick and God would answer with His miracle working power.

On this particular evening, when I asked the crowd as to

how many of them needed a miracle from God, almost everybody present stood up. I asked the crowd to line up along the walls of the sanctuary in single file. The "healing line" formed and snaked all the way around the walls of the sanctuary. I stood on the edge of the platform and asked the people to pass in front of me in single file. As they walked past me I would lay my hands upon them in the name of the Lord Jesus. This is how I ministered that particular evening.

There was a lady in a wheelchair in the "healing line." When she reached me I asked her, "What is wrong with you lady?" She replied, "I cannot stand or walk. I have been totally paralyzed from the waist down and have been in this wheelchair for 11 years. I do not even have any sensation in my legs or my feet. If you touched or pinched my legs I would not feel a thing."

"So what do you want Jesus to do for you?" I queried.

"I want to be healed," she replied.

I then asked her, "God can heal you instantly, and God can also heal you slowly over a period of time; what do you have faith for in your heart?"

"I have faith for both," she replied. At that moment, I realized that this lady did not have any faith for anything at all. She wished to be healed, but did not have faith for it.

I looked at her, wondering what I should do with her, when I suddenly sensed a faint and indescribable "urge" in my heart. I did not understand what it was, but I sensed that I could not just let go of her, because although she did not have any faith, God wanted to do something for her right there. I could not fully understand it, but there was something that God wanted to do and I did not want to miss it.

I stepped off the platform and stood in front of her, facing her. I laid my hands upon her and prayed for her in the Name of the Lord Jesus. When I was finished, I opened my eyes and said to her, "In the Name of Jesus Christ of Nazareth, rise up and walk!" She tried to get up. Her legs were useless, but her arms were very strong. I watched how she really made an effort to get up out of the wheelchair but couldn't do it.

I laid my hands upon her head, once again, to pray and just happened to look over her head at the long line of people behind her. I looked, but could see nobody there. The people seemed to have vanished. Instead of the people, I saw the wonderful face of our Lord Jesus. He was looking at me with this indescribably beautiful gaze of love in His eyes. Human words would fail me if I would try to describe the wonderful face of our Savior. I stood transfixed, looking at Him, everything stood still; and then I heard the words, "Jesus Christ the same yesterday, today and for ever!" Hearing these words electrified my soul. Something powerful gripped my heart and invaded my very body. I said, "If our Lord Jesus is the same today and He is in this place, it is impossible for this woman not to be healed. It is impossible for her to go back home crippled!"

By then, the Spirit of Faith seemed to have taken hold of my entire being. I was there, but it felt like it wasn't really me. Jesus was everywhere and it felt like I and everything in that place was swallowed up by His Presence. Jesus was there! At that moment, I could not doubt or disbelieve even if I had wanted to. It would be impossible to do so. I was surrounded by and carried away by the presence of God, and in the presence of Jesus impossibilities do not exist and all things are possible!

I asked my interpreter and a young priest, who stood next to me, to pick the lady up from the wheelchair and to hold her up. They did so, her legs dangling lifelessly down to the floor. Then suddenly, scripture after scripture began to pour forth from my mouth. I loudly spoke the Word of God as it came pouring out of my mouth in a torrent.

"Surely he has borne our diseases and has carried our pains, he was wounded for our transgressions he was bruised for our iniquities, the chastisement of our peace was upon them and by his stripes we are healed. Bless the Lord o my soul and all that is within me bless his holy name. Bless the Lord and forget not all his benefits. He forgives all your sins and heals all your diseases..." And on and on the Word came...

I found myself quoting scriptures that I had read but never memorized. It was amazing, and I went on and on speaking the Word of God over the paralyzed woman. Then I saw the power of God begin to move upon her body. A tremor went through her entire body and her legs began to tremble and shake. I saw life come into those lifeless legs.

I asked the interpreter and the priest to let go of her. As they did so, she stood on her own legs with her own strength for the first time in 11 years. She put her hands on my shoulders for balance. I told her to keep them there and to look at me and not at her legs, and we slowly began to walk. I continued speaking out the Word of God.

After some time, she took her hands off my shoulders and slowly walked on her own. I kept on walking with her, loudly speaking the Word of God. I forgot the rest of the crowd and worked with her for over 45 minutes, until she was finally walking perfectly, running, and praising God. She was totally healed. Looking at her one could not imagine that she had been totally paralyzed a short while ago.

As soon as her healing was total and complete, the Spirit of Faith that had so held me in its grip suddenly lifted from me. It was a most amazing sensation. One moment, I could not doubt even if I wanted to, and the next moment I could hardly believe that which I had seen with my very eyes; my mind could not keep up with the immensity of the wonderful miracle that the Lord had done.

This is a classic example of the manifestation of what the Bible in 1 Corinthians 12:9 calls "the Gift of Faith." This is not to be confused with the faith that *"cometh by the hearing... the Word of God"* (Romans 10:17).

The first thing to remember here is that a Gift of the Holy Spirit as in 1 Corinthians 12 is not "owned" by a person. One does not carry a gift around in his pocket and pull it out at whim to lay a prophecy, healing or miracle etc out upon people as one wishes to. The gifts are the Holy Spirit's and He chooses to bring them forth as and when they are needed. We can, of course, develop spiritually to "cooperate" with the Holy Spirit and to be sensitive to His moving, but the gifts are always His. We are merely vehicles or channels of His Grace and Glory.

In situations such as this when we have stretched our faith as far as we can, God brings forth His Faith and makes up for that which is lacking. This is called the Gift of Faith. All glory and praise to our Lord Jesus! He sends His faith and makes the impossible possible. God is so good that He goes way above and beyond that which man has faith for. His Grace far overshadows our limited faith. Let us be thankful that He does not always just mete unto us according to our paltry faith, but that He gives way above and beyond that which we can ask or imagine, according to His Grace, which is far greater than our faith could ever be.

"Now unto him that is able to do exceeding abundantly above all that we ask or think, according to the power that worketh in us, Unto him be glory in the church by Christ Jesus throughout all ages, world without end. Amen." Ephesians 3:20-21

Chapter 10

THE BRAIN-DAMAGED LITTLE GIRL

PHALOMBE, MALAWI

It was my very first trip to Malawi, a beautiful, warm, friendly but impoverished nation in South-central Africa. We had just finished a crusade in the capital city of Lilongwe and had a couple of days break before our next crusade which was scheduled to be held in the city of Blantyre. I had looked forward to the two days of rest that I was getting between the crusades, but then some pastors approached me and pleaded with me to go and preach in a couple of very far and remote villages. These villages had never been visited by ministers from overseas, and the people there had requested that I come and preach to them. I, therefore, decided to go.

One of these was a small village in the district of Phalombe. Driving from Blantyre on a dirt track through the bush, we finally arrived there after a very long trip. About 500 people had gathered under a large tree to hear the Word of God. They were very poor. They wore threadbare clothes, some were in rags, and very few had shoes. I stood under shade of the tree and preached. There was no electricity in the area and thus no PA system; my interpreter and I had to shout really loud in order to be heard by the crowd.

I finished my message and gave the altar call for salvation. Many people responded and received the Lord Jesus. After that I prayed for the sick. Many were healed and came forward to testify of the miracles that the Lord had done for them. This done, we were about to close the meeting when suddenly the Word of the Lord came to me.

The Lord spoke to me very clearly, and I had no doubt that I was hearing from God. He said, "There is a woman here who has a child at home that is severely brain-damaged and mentally handicapped. I want you to call the woman out and pray for her child. I shall heal the child."

I wished that it had rather been a Word of Knowledge for a bad back, a headache, a cold, or a hurting leg. I certainly had no faith for the healing of a severely brain damaged child…

I said, "Lord, I do not have the faith for this, so I cannot do it."

As clear as if it were a person standing next to me speaking to me, the Lord said, "I did not ask you whether you had the faith or not. I have the faith. I just want you to obey me and do what I tell you to do."

What does one say to that? The Lord should always be obeyed, no matter how one "feels." I felt scared, small and inadequate, and I looked around me. By now, the pastors and the people were all looking at me, wondering why I was not saying or doing anything.

I then decided to go against my lack of faith and feelings of inadequacy, and just obey God.

I said to the crowd, "There is a woman here. You are in the back of the crowd on my left. You have a child at home born severely brain damaged and mentally handicapped. Come to the front. God wants to heal your child!"

Sure enough, a woman rose to her feet in the general area of the crowd that I was pointing to. She walked up to the front and stood before me. Tears streamed down her cheeks.

I was afraid, my heart was pounding and my throat felt dry. I was all too aware of my inadequacy and lack of faith for such a massive miracle. This was definitely way above my league. I was doing this just to obey Jesus. It was 100% Jesus and 0% me. He was the Healer, and I was just the man who happened to be there, picked out by Him to be the one to speak it forth and for His power to flow through. But why me? I had no faith at all!

I looked at the woman, then at the crowd. I am ashamed to say what happened next. It suddenly struck me that when God does an outstanding miracle He gets the glory, but if a person is not healed the preacher is the one who gets blamed for not being anointed enough. Not having any faith, I, therefore, decided that the blame in this case should be "collective" and not wholly on me!

I said, "I would like all the pastors to come forward and join me!" I said this knowing that in Malawi almost everybody who has been a Christian for a few years loves to call himself "Pastor." A horde of men responded. They all got up and came and stood before me.

I did all this because of the unbelief that had gripped my mind. I did this because when it would later turn out that the child was not healed, I could play the classic "Charismatic blame game" and say, "Well, one of the people who prayed with me did not have faith, that is why the girl was not healed!"

I then took out my handkerchief and held it in my hand

together with everybody else around me and prayed, "Father, I ask you to saturate this piece of cloth now with the presence and the power of your Holy Spirit. I ask that when this cloth is laid upon the child, the child shall be totally healed and delivered. In the Name of our Lord Jesus. Amen."

I handed the handkerchief to the mother and instructed her to put it upon her child when she got home. Secretly, I was hoping that she would lose it somewhere! After this, we closed the meeting and drove back to Blantyre, to the Mount Soche Hotel where I was staying. During the drive, I reflected on the events of the day. I still did not "feel" any faith concerning the child's healing. I had acted against my own doubts and had just obeyed the Lord. I had done what He had told me to do. The Lord had spoken to me rather emphatically when He had told me to pray for the child, and I could honestly say that I had obeyed Him, even though there was absolutely none of my "personal faith" involved in the matter.

Two days later, the main pastor who served as my interpreter came to see me at the hotel early in the morning. His face was flushed with excitement, and he was beaming from ear to ear.

"Pastor Christopher!" he shouted in excitement. "Praise the Lord! God has done a wonderful miracle! Hallelujah!"

He then began to tell me the news that he had just received from the village where we had been two days earlier. Some of the local pastors from there had gotten very excited and had traveled down to Blantyre to tell him the news... the news that the woman had taken the prayer cloth home and put it upon her brain-damaged daughter when she had put her to bed that evening. When the little girl woke up the next morning, she was perfectly normal, totally healed. God had even altered the deformed features of the child's face so that the mother had hardly recognized her at first. God had done a most amazing miracle!

I was broken, humbled. This was 100% Jesus and 0% Christopher Alam. I praised the Lord, but had to come to grips with the fact that God in His Grace had gone past my unbelief and done it not because of me, but in spite of me. Thank God for His Grace, He wanted to fulfill His purpose and chose to use me in spite of my own gross unbelief!

The news of this miracle spread like wildfire through that region. Many people came to Jesus, and we were able to instantly plant 5 new churches in the area.

This was a "strategic" miracle. One mighty miracle from God had turned the spiritual balance of power in the whole region upside down. The Lord Jesus was known, loved, and worshiped more than He had ever been before in that region.

I learned a big lesson from this; to never interpret what God wants me to do by what I "feel" in my human mind or emotions. God, at times, wants to do things that are far beyond our capacity to understand. If my mind cannot grasp the immensity of what God wants to do, I should never give any room to the spirit of unbelief, but just shut up and obey Him anyway!

He is the Lord. His Grace is far greater than we can ever comprehend. We, though imperfect, are His vessels; the least we can do is to obey Him unquestioningly even if it is beyond our understanding. It is best to do what He bids us, not making any room for unbelief, and to obey Him unquestioningly, even if is beyond us.

That is when He can do things far greater than we could ask or think! Blessed be His Name for ever!

Chapter 11

THE CRIPPLED HINDU RSS LEADER

JEODEGRI, ORISSA, INDIA

Orissa in Northern India is one of the staunchest Hindu regions in the entire nation. This is supposedly the home of "Jagannath" (Sanskrit for "The prince of the world"), one of the major deities of Hinduism's 330 million gods and goddesses. This is the state where Hindu fanatics have often burned churches and brutally persecuted and even killed Christians. A few years ago, Australian missionary, Graham Staines and his two small sons were attacked and burned alive in their jeep by Hindu extremists.

My story is from the late 80s. I was ministering extensively in Orissa at that time, holding open air crusades and planting churches in unreached areas in the interior of the state. A Pentecostal gentleman, who was an officer in the government of India's department of agriculture, came to see me when I was holding a crusade in the city of Bhubaneshwar. He told me that he had been working in the remote regions of Phulbani district of Orissa and had led the inhabitants of four villages to the Lord and planted churches in these four villages. This had upset the local leaders of the RSS, a nationwide movement of very violent Hindu extremists who desire the eradication of

Christianity from India and have very often killed Christians and burnt their homes and churches.

The RSS alleged that this man had paid the villagers money to convert to Christianity. They demanded that the government investigate the issue. In response to this, government officials were sent to the four villages to investigate. The villagers told them, "We were all impoverished, drunkards, and our women were prostitutes. The government or the RSS never came to help us. Now Jesus Christ has transformed our lives and these people who never cared for us are here to complain!"

The government investigated and finally absolved the Christian official of all wrongdoing. The leaders of the RSS were furious at this. Armed RSS men went on a rampage in Phulbani district and attacked Christians. They burnt down around 16 churches. I was told that many Christians had been severely beaten and it was also rumored that some Christians in remote villages had even been killed.

I also read in an international newspaper that the Indian government, in an effort to defuse the situation, had stepped in and banned all religious gatherings in that area. I, the wild evangelist and troublemaker that I was, decided to go to the area where all this was going on for an open-air crusade. I have never liked the easy and beaten track of traditional crusade evangelism; going to places like Madras, Nairobi, and Manila where one huge but fruitless crusade follows another, with the very same people getting "saved" again and again. On the contrary, I have always enjoyed going to preach in "tough" places to stir things up by the power of God, and to see how God can turn things upside down and destroy the devil's grip upon the people there.

I was also emboldened by what had happened in Canadian

evangelist Roy Durman's recent crusade in another city in Orissa. Rev. Durman is a soft spoken, gentle, and elderly man filled with Pentecostal Fire. An armed company-strength group of the RSS marched into his crusade in military formation and stood at the back waiting for orders from their leaders to attack.

Rev. Durman's interpreter was terrified and whispered into his ear "The RSS is here, pastor!" Rev. Durman raised one hand up in the air and began to pray. As he prayed, the power of God fell upon the crowd. Thousands of people began to fall down upon the ground like dominos, including the RSS thugs in the back. They hit the ground hard. Frightened out of their wits, they jumped up to their feet and started to run from there like scared rabbits. Terrified, they bolted as fast as their legs could carry them, shouting, "Their God is killing us! Their God is killing us!"

News of this incident spread fast. I was holding a crusade in another city in Orissa during that time and I was told this the next day by pastors who had attended Rev. Durman's crusade. I am a certified troublemaker for Jesus and I like such stories! This helped me decide that I must go to the Phulbani area for a crusade and stir things up there.

The crusade was prepared by our ministry partners in Orissa State. I flew in from Sweden with an 8-man team of eager students from the Bible school where I was a teacher. We flew in to Delhi, then on to Calcutta, and finally to Bhubaneshwar. In Bhubaneshwar, we got on a bus. After an 8 hour ride over rough and bumpy roads, we finally arrived in the jungles of Phulbani. It was dark when we finally reached our destination, the outskirts of a small town called Jeodegri. This is where the crusade would be held. We slept in an ancient and primitive "Mission House," which in times long ago, during the days of the British Raj, used to house British missionaries. Overrun by massive spiders, the place could be best described as on its way to fast becoming a crumbling ruin. There was no electricity or running water. Washing up and bathing was done outdoors next to a deep well from which one drew water with a rope and bucket and poured it over oneself. The food there could be at best described as "extremely nasty."

Desperate for some good food, I bought a live goat for my team of Swedes and myself. My plan was to barbeque it. The goat, of course, was "on the hoof" and had to be slaughtered and dressed first, so I took a knife and sharpened it for the task. My Swedish team, spiritual warriors (It must be noted that these people prided themselves as being "Spiritual Vikings") who prayed shouting loudly at the devil in the prayer room, all gathered around me enthusiastically to watch, cameras in hand. The time for slaughter came, but I found the goat to be most uncooperative; after all, its life was at stake and it wasn't too eager to become meat for the table. I got some volunteers to hold it down while I began the grisly task of slaughtering it by slitting open its throat, the only way I knew how to. When the poor goat's blood began to spurt out all over the place, four tall, strong, strapping Swedish Spiritual Viking Warriors promptly fainted and fell down upon the ground. It was quite a sight!

I thought of the missionaries of old who would leave the comforts of Europe and America to preach the Gospel in heathen lands far away. They would carry their belongings in coffins instead of suitcases, because they were willing to pay any price, even laying down their lives, to get the Gospel out to far away nations. Growing up, I saw many ancient cemeteries with the graves of missionaries, often entire families buried side by side. What a price they had been willing to pay to get the message of Salvation out to sinners!

Being in that old crumbling "Mission House" stirred up the depths of our spirits, and we realized that we were walking in the footsteps of men and women of God who had paid such a price sowing the precious seed of the Gospel in such a difficult and heathen land. Now, it was our turn. We were there, sent by God over two centuries after these first pioneers, treading on the very soil where the blessed feet of those brave men and women of old had once trod. We were there to reap with joy where they had sown the precious seed of the Gospel so long ago, and with so many tears. The harvest was ripe and God had sent us to the wild region of Phulbani to preach the Gospel of Jesus. He had sent us to proclaim the total victory of Jesus over all the powers of Satan.

This was the first ever Gospel crusade held in the area, and many had come expecting great things from God. The crusade was to be held in the daytime, because most of the people had to walk through the surrounding jungles teeming with dangerous wild animals in order to get to the crusade from their homes, and then back home again. Many had come from afar, carrying their sick relatives and friends with them, and were sleeping under the trees and had decided to stay there until God touched them.

There was such faith and expectation there that it broke us, humbled us. The expectations of the impoverished people who had gathered there in Jeodegri were far greater than my faith.

This is a most important thing to understand. When God does great miracles, Christians often make the mistake of giving credit to the minister who God uses at the time. The truth (at least that is what I have experienced in my life) is that over 90% of the miracles that God does through my ministry are because of the faith and the expectations of the people. Less than 10% is because of the gifting of God upon my life. I am totally dependent upon the people seeing Jesus through my preaching. If I can only get them to the point where they only "see" Jesus and don't see me any more, THAT is when miracles begin to flow! It is Jesus and Him alone. We are merely servants and conduits of His power. Yes, God will give us all things, but He will only glorify His Son Jesus. He will never share His glory with another.

Yes, I believe in the boldness and confidence that comes by faith; but true boldness, confidence, and faith spring forth only from the place of brokenness, when we realize and say that "without Jesus I am nothing!" Once we come to that place of death, we rise to life, where we can say, "But I am not without Jesus, I live in Him, and He lives in me. Because I am nothing, He is everything in and through me!"

Now, THAT is true confidence in God. We place no confidence in the flesh. That is why we must live in the place of brokenness and dying to self everyday, so that we may also daily live in the resurrected, victorious life of Christ. O, what a glorious paradox! THIS is the place where God can cause His power to flow through us and around us, bringing life and healing… And then we can say, "All glory to Jesus, because He alone is worthy!"

The crusade started with an explosion of God's power. As I was preaching the first day, there was a loud clap of thunder and it began to rain very heavily. Our PA system was immediately switched off, and within moments we were totally soaked. But amazingly, the people stayed on. My team and I waded into the crowd and began to lay hands upon the sick. All kinds of miracles began to happen all over the crowd. Blind eyes were opened, and crippled people got up and walked. Then, as quickly as it started, the rain stopped. By then, the field was a sea of water and mud.

I found a dry spot, placed a table there, stood atop the table and preached. The Holy Ghost moved over the people. God was all over the place! It was indescribable.

On the second day, the crowd had doubled. We had a good crusade service with thousands coming to Jesus and many being healed from different diseases and infirmities.

Here I want to skip the details and go to the "Divine Fireworks" of the third day. A huge crowd had gathered to hear the Gospel. The presence of God was tangible, and one could feel it in the air... I preached the Word of God and invited sinners to receive Jesus as their Lord and Savior. Thousands responded. Then, I began to pray for the sick *en masse*.

First were the deaf... many deaf people received their hearing as God healed them. Then the blind... people began to scream as they saw blind people around them receive their sight. Such is the wonder working power of our Lord Jesus!

And then I prayed for the lame, the crippled.

The power of God fell, and right in front of me I saw several lame people get up and walk. I saw a mother pick up her son who was born lame, and the boy began to walk. People were shouting and praising God all over the place.

Then suddenly, I heard a lot of noise and commotion from the back of the multitude. The crowd began to part and make way for a man making his way to the front from the very back of the crowd. He was walking with his arms held aloft, shouting, "Jesus is Alive! Jesus is Alive." People were shouting and crying.

When he reached the front he stepped up upon the platform

and grabbed the microphone from my interpreter. The interpreter looked terrified. The crowd suddenly fell silent. The man now faced the crowd and shouted into the microphone in Hindi, "Yesu Masih ki Jai!" which means, "Jesus is Victorious!" He shouted this again and again. The crowd, upon seeing and hearing this man shouting the praises of God, came unglued. People were shouting and praising God at the top of their voices. Some were screaming, others were running and jumping. In moments, the place went from order to total chaos.

The man now stepped off the platform and started walking away, shouting, "Jesus is Alive! Jesus is Alive!" Thousands of people detached themselves from the crowd and excitedly began to follow the man, shouting and yelling at the top of their voices as he walked away praising God with his hands held high.

I had never seen anything like this before. After the service, I noticed the unusual excitement among the pastors and asked them about what had happened. It was then that they told me this amazing story...

This man who was walking around and shouting "Jesus is Alive!" was a top leader in the Hindu-extremist RSS. He was born crippled and could only stand and move with a pair of large and robust crutches. He was the leader of the group that had terrorized Christians and burnt down churches. He had such a fearsome reputation for brutality that when Christian women would see him coming hobbling on his crutches leading his gang of RSS thugs, they would pick up their babies and run into the jungles. They would rather face the wild animals instead of this man.

He had heard about our crusade and that Hindus were coming to Christ. This had made him furious, and he had decided to go and see for himself. He had come to the crusade in a jeep with his RSS thugs following in a bus. He had stood at the back of the crowd and watched the service livid with anger. Soon, he and his gang would make their move and spread mayhem and destruction.

And then came the time when I began to pray for the crippled and the lame. Totally unexpectedly, God touched him right where he stood. The power of Jesus Christ surged through his body like high-voltage electricity. His followers standing around him saw him shake and tremble violently. Then they saw his crutches go flying in different directions. He was standing on his own legs without support for the first time in his life. He was amazed, shocked, and did not really grasp what had happened to him. Still shocked, he lifted his hands up in the air and began to walk forward through the crowd, shouting again and again, "Jesus is Alive! Jesus is Alive!" The people turned around and saw who it was. Stupefied and awestruck, they made way for him as he walked towards the platform.

"Jesus is alive!" Yes truly, in this age of gross unbelief, when even church people doubt and question the miracle-working power of God, thank God for a Hindu-extremist who found out that the Jesus Christ he had hated was alive. Not only was He alive, but He also loved him enough to heal him when he was so far from God and so full of the devil.

What a wonderful Jesus we serve! There is none other like Him!

I was back in Orissa State a year later. The agricultural officer whose ministry had stirred up all the trouble came to see me. He reported that the RSS leader's healing and salvation at our crusade had unleashed revival in the Phulbani district. Over 70 churches had been started in the wake of our crusade, and churches that were dead and dying had received a fresh infusion of life and were experiencing a move of God.

There is a heartwarming end to this story. Twelve years after this incident, I was teaching at my friends Rev. Sam and Dawn Taylor's Bible school in south India. They had 700 students from all over India and from Nepal that year, and the classes were interpreted simultaneously into 14 different languages. Students from that school go out all over India and plant churches in many difficult places.

One morning whilst teaching, I encouraged the students, telling them that we should never fear what man or the devil might want to do to hinder us from preaching the Gospel to sinners. I told them that the RSS was nothing before the power of God, and that He who lives in us is greater than he that is in the world. I then related the story of the crusade in Jeodegri 12 years ago, and about how God had dealt with the RSS leader and brought revival.

After the class was over, a student in his early 20s walked up to me with tears running down his cheeks. He said, "Pastor Christopher, I was there! I was a little 10 year old boy and my mother took me to that meeting. I sat on my mother's lap in front of the platform. I remember all the people and all the miracles. A boy I knew who was born crippled got up and began to walk. I saw how that RSS leader was healed. It was at that meeting that I received Jesus, and then I heard the voice of God calling me to preach the Gospel. That is why I am here to learn the Word of God so that I can go out into ministry." He then added, "There are 10 of us here at this Bible School from Jeodegri. We were all small children, we received Jesus at that meeting, and we all heard the voice of God calling us to service for Him. Now, we are all here together, preparing to go out to serve God."

Tears came to my eyes. I looked at this young man, hugged him and we cried. I was greatly encouraged... Yes, it was all worth it. All the sacrifices we missionaries and our families have to make to get the Gospel out to the lost; it is worth it all!

One day, we shall go Home to be with Jesus. We shall march in through the gates of Glory. What a joyous day that will be! We shall stand there rejoicing before the Throne of the Lamb together with millions of souls redeemed from every tribe, nation, and tongue... the fruit of the labors of missionaries and of those who sent them out, prayed for them, supported them... all dressed in white, all washed in the Blood of the Lamb!

Yes, the price paid is worth it all!

Hallelujah to Jesus the Son of God!

> *"For I am not ashamed of the gospel of Christ: for it is the power of God unto salvation to every one that believeth; to the Jew first, and also to the Greek."* Romans 1:16

Chapter 12

MIRACLES AND DELIVERANCE

ESIKHAWINI, SOUTH AFRICA

This story is from the early 90s, the time when South Africa was going through the painful final birth pangs of freedom from apartheid. Violence raged across the land; members of the African Nation Congress and the Inkatha Freedom Party fought pitched battles in almost every town of the country, killing one another. News of the wholesale slaughter of humanity all across South Africa shocked the entire world.

During those days, my team asked Jonas Hjalmarsson, a Swedish missionary ministering in the Kwa-Zulu Natal Province of South Africa, "Is there a really bad place that you can think of where we could go and make a difference?"

Jonas's answer was, "Esikhawini."

Esikhawini lies close to the coast in Northern Natal, about 90 kms north of Durban and near the well-known towns of Empangeni and Richard's Bay. Esikhawini was, at that time, one of the bloodiest places in South Africa. The ANC (African National Congress) and Inkatha were fighting and killing each other with guns, "pangas" (machetes), and spears. For a white man to go to Esikhawini was considered suicidal, because it was reputed that no white man going there would return alive.

My Director of Operations for Africa at that time, Mats Svanstrom, a blond Swede, went to Esikhawini and contacted the local pastors in town. They were glad, albeit shocked and surprised, to see a white man dare to venture into Esikhawini. It was agreed by all that Esikhawini was in dire need of the Gospel message, and the dates for the projected crusade were decided upon.

There was only one open field in Esikhawini suitable for a crusade and that was right next door to the ANC workers' hostel. This field was the scene of regular battles fought between the ANC and the Inkhata, and one can only imagine how much blood had soaked the soil of that field.

After meeting with the pastors, Mats went to the ANC hostel to inform their leaders about the crusade. The ANC, being an organization with strong communist leanings, did not like the idea of a Gospel crusade being held next to their stronghold and warned Mats that they "could not guarantee our safety" if we came to preach there.

In the meantime, people were being slaughtered in Esikhawini every single day. Violence was everywhere and people were deathly terrified to go out of their homes after sunset. Armed gangs roamed the streets after dark, killing and raping with impunity, and everybody stayed indoors as a consequence.

Our crusade was to start on a Tuesday night, and on the Sunday night, two days before the crusade, four people were killed on the very field where we would be preaching the Gospel.

The crusade started with a handful of brave souls in attendance. These were the few whose hunger for the Gospel outweighed their fear of the murderers who prowled the night.

On the second night, the leading "Sangoma" or witch of Esikhawini showed up at the crusade. Sangomas are highly feared and respected in South Africa. This particular Sangoma had a fearsome reputation for her occult powers. She was greatly feared by the people of Esikhawini and those who were present at the service were quite surprised to see her there. As I preached about Jesus that night, the evil spirits in her began to manifest themselves. She fell on the ground screaming, writhing, and rolling around. Terrified people ran for cover. When I saw her on the ground, I jumped down from the platform and ran towards her to cast the devils out of her. As I commanded the demons to come out of her in the Mighty Name of the Lord Jesus, they began to leave her, powerless before that Name that God has exalted far above every other name.

After sometime, when all the demons had left her, she came to rest with a deep sigh and opened her eyes. She was free, totally free! She then gave her life wholeheartedly to the Lord Jesus. Everybody who saw this was amazed.

Word of this spread through Esikhawini like wildfire and generated much excitement throughout the town. The next day, we sent people to her house to clean it out of every demonic influence. She handed over all her charms and artifacts used in the practice of witchcraft. All these things were thrown into a huge oil drum and burnt at the crusade ground before that evening's crusade service.

The crusade started on the third evening with about 300 people in attendance. I was somewhat disappointed as we had come all the way from Zimbabwe, expecting thousands to attend the crusade but so few came. This was our third night, and we were already halfway through the crusade.

Then something happened that cracked the whole town open for the Gospel.

In the little crowd that night, was a mother who had carried her 10 year old son to the crusade. The boy had a powerful spell of witchcraft cast upon him some years back (whether it was by the "Sangoma" who had been set free the previous night, I don't know). After that, the boy had become totally paralyzed from head to toe. His eyes stared out into space, blank, expressionless, and he couldn't or wouldn't hear or speak. In other words, he appeared to be in a totally vegetative state. Almost the whole town knew about this boy and that his condition was the result of witchcraft. This is a very common thing in Africa.

His mother laid him down on the grass and stood listening to the Word of God. As I was preaching the Gospel message about Jesus, she felt a little hand on her arm. She turned to see who it was and was shocked to see her son standing next to her holding her arm. She was speechless. He was looking up at her. "Mamma, where are we?" were his first words. "We are in church," she replied, still in shock. She then realized that the Lord had done a wonderful miracle for her. She brought him up to the platform to testify of what the Lord had done for her son. A loud shout went up from the crowd when they saw the mother and her son standing, smiling, and talking. They began to cheer and to praise God.

This was the miracle that broke Satan's stranglehold on Esikhawini. First the Sangoma, now this little boy, both set free from the devil's power. The whole town was stirred up. The next night thousands packed the field to hear the Gospel. Even the ANC men in their hostel just 20 yards behind the platform came out to their balconies and were shouting "Hallelujah" and loud praises to God. Many of them later came out and joined the crowd and gave their lives to Jesus. White people came from the nearby towns of Richard's Bay and Empangeni to hear the Gospel.

The biggest murderers during those terrible times in South Africa were armed thugs of the so-called Inkatha Freedom Party. For some reason, they were killing not only white people, but their fellow Africans too. These people were responsible for most of the bloodshed in Esikhawini, and they did not, at all, like what we were doing; so on Saturday night, they showed up at the crusade. Their motives were not entirely pure, because some of them threatened our workers with violence. I was told of this just before the service.

That night, as I preached the gospel, I decided that this was a "now or never" moment. It was do or die. Jesus or the devil. Victory or defeat. I then went straight out and preached hard, real hard. I took time to lay it out on the Inkatha murderers. Pointing at them, I preached to them that they were not worthy to be respected because they were nothing more than murderers who were going to Hell and would burn there forever. This, I informed them, put them in a category lower than the worms that crawled in the dirt. I told them that I did not fear them because my God who lives in me is far greater than the devil that was in them. My heart was pounding. If I had to die, I'd die there. I was reminded of an old Arabic proverb, "It is better to die like a lion than to live like a dog." So, I decided to press on.

The crowd was shocked, stunned, fearing what the Inkatha would do. I finally told them, "Listen you murderers, you sons of the devil; you may not like me for telling you the truth. Tonight you might hate me, but one day you'll thank me because I am giving you a break. This is the only break you will ever receive in your miserable lives; and here it is: Get down on your knees! Repent and give your life to Jesus, and your sins shall be forgiven! You shall become sons of God and live for ever in His presence. If you don't come to Jesus, you are lost for ever. So what will it be? Heaven or Hell? Jesus or the devil?

The crowd was quiet, stunned. Then suddenly someone shouted, "Hallelujah!" Then another person began to clap his hands, then another and another until everybody was shouting and praising God. At the same time, I watched the Inkatha thugs who had threatened us get down on their knees one after the other, repenting of their terrible sins, coming to Jesus and receiving that most precious gift that only Jesus, the Son of God can give.

The Lord had done a great work. Satan's hold was broken, the people of Esikhawini could hear the Gospel and we reaped a massive harvest of souls for Jesus!

"For our gospel came not unto you in word only, but also in power, and in the Holy Ghost..." 1 Thessalonians 1:5

Chapter 13

GRACIELA'S DELIVERANCE

ROSARIO, ARGENTINA

This is not really a story of physical healing, but a wonderful testimony of deliverance from the power of Satan. This happened during my very first crusade in Argentina, which was held in the city of Rosario, about 200 miles away from Buenos Aires.

This crusade shook Rosario in a big way. Huge multitudes were coming to hear the Gospel every night, and the power of the Holy Ghost manifested mightily in every service. Many were coming to Jesus, God was doing amazing miracles of healing, and many people were being set free from the power of Satan.

The reason that so many people were being delivered from demons in Rosario is due to the fact that Rosario was a hotbed of occult and satanic practices. The practice of witchcraft was a widespread phenomenon, and the city was infested with "curanderos" or occult healers, i.e. witches and warlocks who claim to be able to heal the sick through occult powers.

It is a known fact that God has given to the Lord Jesus the Name that is above every other name, and that at the mention of the Name of Jesus Christ of Nazareth every evil spirit has to flee. The Name of Jesus is mighty over every kind of disease and evil spirit that exists today or has ever existed in times past. They have to flee at the very mention of that majestic Name. Because of this, every service in our crusade in Rosario was also a confrontation between the power of the Lord Jesus and the powers of darkness. In each case, Satan and his cohort of spirits had to flee, and those that were bound by them were set totally free by the invincible power of the Lord Jesus Christ.

These confrontations took place in every service. As I would preach and pray every night, scores, sometimes hundreds of demon-possessed people would fall to the ground screaming. We had an army of ushers and crusade workers who would pick them off the ground where they lay screaming and writhing and carry them to the "deliverance tent" behind the preaching platform. Some of the spirits were really violent and it took several strong men to subdue the demon possessed and to carry them away.

The "deliverance tent" was a huge rented circus tent manned by fifty Pentecostal women who were praying, shouting, and singing Blood songs. This was the kind of atmosphere that any devil in his right mind would run from! The tent was filled, every night, by writhing and screaming people who were getting demons cast out of them in the mighty Name of Jesus Christ.

One day, while resting in my hotel room, I received a call from the hotel receptionist. He said that a gentleman was waiting in the lobby and wanted to see me. I went downstairs and saw a strong and burly Argentinean man waiting for me. He was weeping like a baby. I asked him what the matter was and between heart-wracking sobs he told me the following story:

"My wife has been quite ill for sometime. I took her to many doctors, but nobody has been able to help her. This has gone on for so long. We have only one child, Graciela (name changed to protect her identity), our 17 year old daughter. We are a very close-knit family, and my daughter could not bear to see her mother suffer this way; so she, on her own initiative, went to a "curandero" (occult healer) to get help for her mother. Not long after this visit to the "curandero", demons began to manifest in her. She is now totally possessed by devils and has lost her mind. She has been crying and screaming for the past ten days. None of us have been able to sleep the past three nights because she has been up and screaming day and night. We have taken her to the crusade but nothing has helped. Could you please help us?"

I assured him that I would do what I could for his daughter, and asked him to bring her back to the crusade that night.

A huge multitude came to the crusade to hear the Gospel that night. As the musicians played and the choir sang, I looked over the vast sea of humanity that was clapping, singing, and worshiping God. I spotted a young blonde lady standing right up in the front of the crowd. She stood with her arms folded and glared at me with an incredibly hateful look upon her face.

I instantly knew in my heart that this was Graciela.

I looked at her often as I preached the Gospel that night. She stood still as a statue through the course of my preaching, glaring at me. At the end of the message, I gave an altar call for people to receive Jesus as their Lord and Savior. A forest of hands went up. I began to lead them in the sinners' prayer... "Dear Lord Jesus..."

At the mention of the Name of Jesus, Graciela was suddenly flung violently down onto the ground by the evil spirits that tormented her. She began to writhe, roll, and thrash around violently, screaming horrible, blood-curdling screams...

Some of our ushers ran over to her and picked her up. It took 6 or more strong ushers to carry this violently demon-possessed girl to the prayer tent, where our prayer-warriors began to pray for her.

I carried on with the service, first praying for the sick, and then hearing the testimonies of many people who had been healed by Jesus. This went on for a long time. After closing the service, I ran to the prayer tent to see what had happened to Graciela. Upon entering the large tent, I noticed a great commotion over on one side; a crowd of agitated people had gathered and they were shaking their fists, shouting, and rebuking Satan at the top of their voices. I pushed my way through the crowd and saw Graciela on the ground, rolling, thrashing around, and screaming. Her skirt kept coming up to her waist and some women were occupied solely with keeping her skirt down in place while the rest of the crowd shouted, yelled, and prayed. Some men were trying to pin her down to the ground, but she was throwing them off as if they weighed nothing. The only pastor present stood to one side and watched, doing nothing.

I stepped in and knelt next to her and began to cast the devils out of her. I told the men and the women to let go of her and asked the hysterical crowd to calm down. By now, she was totally wild and out of control, thrashing around with blood-curdling screams. It frightened some of the people who took to their legs and ran for safety. The demons were incredibly strong and violent. I finally had no choice but to sit astride her, like one sits when riding a horse, to keep her under control.

"Come out of her Satan, in the Name of Jesus!" I commanded the demons. In response, Graciela's mouth let forth a stream of unspeakably filthy blasphemies and she clawed at me with her long fingernails.

I continued to minister to her. Then the pastor who was standing and watching the proceedings suddenly began to shout at me that he "did not like my methods." I thought of how easy it is for those who do not give themselves to ministering healing and deliverance to criticize others who do. Those who do not minister along these lines often believe that they know it all and consider themselves to be experts.

I turned to him and said, "Pastor, please be quiet. If there is no unity between you and me here, the devil will stand and laugh at us and we cannot set this girl free." My words seemingly fell on deaf ears and he just went on and on shouting at me. I then got up and said to him, "Fine. If you can do a better job than me, please come and take over!" I then turned around and walked away. The pastor just stood glued to where he stood and stared at me as I left, doing nothing to help Graciela.

As I was outside the tent and getting into the car that would take me back to the hotel, Graciela ran out and grabbed me. Holding me tight, she cried, "Please don't leave me with these devils! Please don't go away!"

I, however, felt that it was too far gone by then. That pastor had ruined everything. He had, by now, come out of the tent and stood glaring at me while the girl pleaded with me not to leave her in that state. I felt that I could not do any more for her in the present situation, so I got into the car and left.

The next day was Sunday, and I was scheduled to preach in one of the local churches. As this was just one of the 40 churches participating in the crusade and they wanted everybody to go to their own home church, they had not announced the name of the church where I would be speaking that morning.

The service started, and when it was finally time for me to preach I walked up on to the platform. There were hundreds of people in the congregation. I read from the Bible and began to preach about Elijah and Elisha; about how Elisha followed Elijah. I then noticed Graciela, sitting between her parents about 5 or 6 rows down from the front. She had a dark look upon her face and sat with her arms crossed. She looked down at the floor much of the time and would look up to glare at me every now and then. She would also often get up and run out of the building. Her parents would then run after her and bring her back inside. This happened several times during my message.

Finally, at the end of the message I gave an invitation. I asked those who wanted to follow Jesus as Elisha had followed Elijah to come to the altar. A couple hundred people came forward. I was surprised to see Graciela among them. The Spirit of God must have touched her, I surmised.

I began to pray from the platform, at the same time keeping an eye on Graciela. Then something happened. Graciela gently fell down on the floor under the power of God.

I then saw something most amazing begin to happen. Graciela's face began to glow as she lay on the floor; literally glow, with light emanating from her face. I had seen this only once before, on the face of a young woman who was caught up in the Spirit in the darkened vestry of a Roman Catholic church in Lublin, Poland. Graciela's face literally glowed with the Glory of God. Such a miraculous manifestation of God's power is hard to describe in words, except that looking at her face was like looking at a glowing light bulb.

I watched, the people standing around her watched. Her face glowed for about 15 minutes whilst she lay on the floor. There was an expression of serenity over her visage. Then the glow slowly subsided. Graciela opened her eyes. Her very face seemed to have been transformed. The darkness was gone; her demeanor was now full of light. She began to smile, laugh, weep, and praise God at the same time. Bounding up the steps to the platform, she began to hug and kiss me and all the pastors around me. The whole congregation erupted into loud praises unto God.

Graciela was free!

I went back to Argentina 10 years later in 1998 and preached at a crusade in Rosario and in meetings at Graciela's home church. Graciela was there, beautiful and full of life. She was 27 and a successful attorney in Rosario.

This is what our Lord Jesus can do!

"I beheld Satan as lightning fall from heaven. Behold, I give unto you power to tread on serpents and scorpions, and over all the power of the enemy: and nothing shall by any means hurt you. Notwithstanding in this rejoice not, that the spirits are subject unto you; but rather rejoice, because your names are written in heaven."
Luke 10:18-20

107

Chapter 14

THE MOTHER WHO
REFUSED TO GIVE UP

MUTARE, ZIMBABWE

This story is from my first crusade in Mutare, a city up in the beautiful Eastern Highlands of Zimbabwe. Mutare lies up on top of a 5000 ft high escarpment overlooking the jungles of Mozambique.

We were holding our crusade in a stadium in the Sakuva township, the largest township in the area. Massive crowds were coming out to hear the Gospel preached every night. The Spirit of the Lord was moving mightily with huge multitudes giving their lives to the Lord Jesus.

It was on the second evening that I noticed a woman who stood in the front of the crowd carrying a little boy on her back, tied in a "chitenge" sheet in the African fashion. I spotted her the next evening as well. In fact, she stood at the same spot every evening.

I noticed that at every single service, when I would pray for the sick *en masse*, she would undo the chitenge and take the little boy off her back and try to get him to stand on his legs. Every time she would do this I would see the little boy's paralyzed legs crumple lifelessly under him and he would fall down on the ground. When the service would end, I would watch how she would pick up the child, put him on her back, and walk away from the crusade.

My heart went out to the woman and the little boy, and I asked my team to find out more about her. It turned out that the little boy was her son, 10 years old and born totally paralyzed. She lived 10 kilometers (6.2 miles) away and would walk that distance to the crusade every day, carrying her son on her back. She would get there early so that she could get a place to stand in the front of the crowd. After the crusade she would walk the same distance back home, carrying her crippled son on her back.

She was full of faith, and she was determined not to give up until her son was healed.

Evening after evening I would watch her put her son down to walk. My heart would beat hard in anticipation and excitement, but he would fall down, his legs still paralyzed and lifeless. Then my own heart would sink in disappointment, but I knew that she would be back. She would be standing at the same spot the next evening, determined and not giving up, refusing to be disappointed at God and still steadfastly trusting Him.

Every evening, at the end of every service, the people would rejoice, sing, and dance. And why shouldn't they? After all, multitudes were receiving Jesus; the deaf were hearing, the blind were seeing, and the lame were walking and leaping for joy. Yet in the middle of all this, I found it hard to really join in the rejoicing, because my heart was set on that little boy and his mother.

I found myself pleading with God for this boy, asking Him to heal him. Every evening, when I would preach, I found myself preaching to the mother and child.

Then came the last night of the crusade, and I saw the mother and child at their usual place. I looked up to Heaven and cried out to God... "Lord, this is it! This is the last evening of this crusade. They have come here from so far away every evening... You just have to heal the boy tonight!"

The service started with a sea of people filling the stadium to hear the Word of God. After the singing, the preaching, and the altar call, it was time to pray for the sick. I took one look at the mother and her paralyzed son, went on my knees and prayed with all my heart and soul.

I cried out to God, pouring out my heart to Him in prayer. When I had said the final "amen" I instructed the people to begin to check themselves and to do something that they could not do before. People began to drop their crutches, walking and running, deaf and blind people were healed, the crowd was shouting and rejoicing; but my eyes were watching that mother and her paralyzed son.

I watched as she undid the "chitenge" cloth in which she had tied him to her back. She took him in her hands and put him down to walk. My heart beat faster and harder. This was the moment! I watched as he stood and... No! His legs crumpled lifelessly under him and he fell down to the ground.

I was disappointed, heartbroken, crushed.

A long line of people who had been healed came up and testified from the platform about the great things that God had done for them. There was much cheering, shouting, and rejoicing. I kept up a brave face through all this, but inside I was heartbroken because of the little boy.

After the last testimony, the worship team and band began to sing a rousing chorus, praising God for the things that He had done. The sea of humanity that covered the whole field erupted into dancing to the lively African beat. They were singing, leaping, and dancing with all their might.

I looked at that vast crowd and watched, and then I just happened to look over to where the woman stood. There she was, dancing with all her might. Beside her was her little boy, dancing to keep up with his mother. He was laughing, rejoicing, jumping, waving his little arms, and dancing!

I looked, watched in awe, and fell down on my knees. Tears came to my eyes, and I wept. I cried, broken, joyful. I then stood up, watched that little boy and his mother dance, and began to dance myself, with all my heart!

What a wonderful Jesus we serve! God is a good God, and He is always true and faithful to His Word.

> *"God is not a man, that he should lie; neither the son of man, that he should repent: hath he said, and shall he not do it? or hath he spoken, and shall he not make it good? Behold, I have received commandment to bless: and he hath blessed; and I cannot reverse it."* Numbers 23:19-20

> *"Let us hold fast the profession of our faith without wavering; (for he is faithful that promised)."*
> Hebrews 10:23

When your back is to the wall, remember that it is and it always shall be the way that God has spoken in His Word. Take God's promise, let it be His Rhema Word for you, hold on to it, believe that it is so, and never let go!

The miracle is yours!

Chapter 15

THE MAN HEALED FROM AIDS

HSIPAW, BURMA

Sai Lak is a young man from Kyaukme, a very small town about 22 miles down the Mandalay Road from Hsipaw in Shan State, Burma. He has a sister called Ohn Mar. Sai Lak married a girl who, unbeknownst to him, was infected with the HIV virus. As a result, Sai Lak also contracted HIV. The HIV soon led to full-blown AIDS. Sai Lak's health began to deteriorate. He lost a lot of weight and was soon deathly ill. His mother and sister took him to the Hospital for Infectious Diseases in Mandalay, where it was verified that he indeed was in an advanced stage of AIDS. They told his mother and his sister, "There is nothing that we can do. He is going to die. These are his last days. Just care for him and keep him happy until he dies."

Sai Lak's sister, Ohn Mar, was a strong Christian and would not accept the doctors' verdict. She believed what the Bible taught; that Jesus Christ the miracle worker is the same today as He was in the days when He walked upon this earth. Jesus Christ was, and is even today, the healer of all those who trust in Him. With Him nothing is impossible!

113

Ohn Mar was therefore resolute in her decision to trust God that He would heal her brother. She and her mother heard that I was holding a crusade in Hsipaw, not far away from Kyaukme, and decided to take him there. They decided that they would stay in Hsipaw for the entire week to attend the crusade.

I remember that first evening of the Hsipaw crusade. After I had finished preaching and began to pray for the sick, I saw two ladies walking towards me. They were holding up a skeletal and emaciated man who looked like he was in the very throes of death. He was so weak that he could not stand on his own legs, so the two women were holding him up and in a sense carrying him.

This was the AIDS-stricken Sai Lak, being borne forwards by his mother and sister. Ohn Mar, the sister, said to me, "Saiya (Pastor or teacher in Burmese), please pray for my brother, he is dying of AIDS."

I laid my hands upon the young man in the mighty Name of the Lord Jesus and prayed for him. After I finished praying, his mother and sister took him away.

They were back the next evening and once again asked for prayer. I prayed for him again.

We had arranged free lunches for all the people who had come from out of town to attend the morning teaching seminars. I asked Pastor W, my Director of Operations for Burma, to go and see to it that the people were being properly fed.

As he was going around and checking that everybody was getting enough to eat, he came upon Ohn Mar and her mother seated at a table eating lunch. Sai Lak, the young man, lay on the floor on a straw mat beside the table. Pastor W was also my interpreter in the meetings and had been with me when I had prayed for the young man. Upon seeing him, Sai Lak's mother asked him, "Could you please ask Pastor Christopher to pray for my son again?"

Now, Pastor W had learned about faith and how God's miracle-working power works. I had taught him that God always hears when a believer prays according to God's Word and in the Name of the Lord Jesus Christ. So he responded to the woman's request by asking her, "Mama, do you believe that God hears and heals people when Pastor Christopher prays for them?"

"Yes, He does!" she replied.

"Well then, do you believe that God heard Pastor Christopher when he prayed for your son the first and the second times?"

"Yes, I believe that God heard him," she replied.

"So then, if God has already heard Pastor Christopher, and He heals people when Pastor Christopher prays for them, He has already healed your son! Why does Pastor Christopher then have to pray for him again?"

"Oh... uh... well... yes," they answered somewhat hesitantly.

Pastor W then turned to the young man on the ground. "Why aren't you eating anything, young man?" he asked him.

"I cannot... eat anything... at all, it is... impossible," he replied in a croaking voice that was barely a whisper.

"If God has heard Pastor Christopher and He has touched and healed you, then you better start acting and talking like a healed man instead of a sick man. So get up and eat!" Pastor W said.

The mother and the sister rose from their seats and very gently raised Sai Lak to a sitting position. Slowly and with great difficulty he sat up and put a few grains of rice into his mouth.

"Now eat like this every day and thank God every day that you have been healed!" Pastor W said to Sai Lak.

That was the last that we saw of them. They left that day. Six months later we got a letter from Ohn Mar, Sai Lak's sister. She wrote, "God has healed my brother! The hospital has declared him HIV negative. Tell Pastor Christopher that my brother is perfectly well and that he is even bigger and fatter (To call someone "fat" is a major compliment in Burma!) than him. He is now at a Bible school training to be an evangelist!"

I met Ohn Mar a few years later when she was part of the worship team at a crusade we held in her home town of Kyaukme. She told us that her brother, Sai Lak, was perfectly strong and well and was preaching the Gospel somewhere in Burma.

What a mighty God we serve! With God nothing is impossible, and all things are possible for Him who believes!

"For with God all things are possible." Mark 10:27

Faith always works. Faith overcomes all things.

"And this is the victory that overcometh the world, even

Chapter 16

A LEGACY OF
FAITH AND POWER

There was a time when I used to travel to India very often to preach the Gospel. It was during one of my first trips there that I met an 80 year old man of God who lived in India, an English Pentecostal missionary by the name of Rev. Harold Groves. Rev. Groves, it turned out, was a sort of mentor or "spiritual father" to the famous evangelist TL Osborn.

I found out that Rev. Groves had known and sat under the preaching of legendary men who knew the power of God; men such as Smith Wigglesworth, FF Bosworth, Charles Price, the Jeffries brothers and Howard Carter. I eagerly "milked" Rev. Groves for stories about these great men, and of the great things that he had seen God do. Rev. Groves shared about the amazing miracles that he had seen and shared in depth about faith and about the workings of the miracle power of God.

Through all the things he talked about, there were two phrases that he repeated often, and these stuck in my mind indelibly.

The first was a scripture that he quoted, *"The kingdom of heaven suffereth violence, and the violent take it by force"* (Matthew 11:12).

The second was an expression he had coined, *"You cannot see the power of God until you are willing to pay the price!"*

Then Rev. Groves, in the middle of a story about Smith Wigglesworth, suddenly stopped. He looked at me and said rather irritably, "That is enough! I don't want to talk about this anymore. Go and get some rest young man!"

I was staying in Rev. Groves' house with a friend, and later that day at tea time Rev. Groves looked at us and said, "Everybody asks me about Smith Wigglesworth, about Howard Carter and the others. They are gone and soon I too shall be going upstairs. Today when I was resting, I was thinking of you and your generation. The Lord reminded me of the Scripture *'The glory of this latter house shall be greater than of the former...'* (Haggai 2:9). So what is important is not what people of my generation did, but rather, what you and your generation are going to do with your lives. Are you going to be men of faith, believe God and set the world on fire with the Gospel of Jesus, or are you going to sit around and listen to stories? What are you going to do with your life? That, young man is the challenge right before you!"

When he was finished, my friend and I went down on our knees. I said, "Brother Groves, please pray for us!" With tears rolling down his face, Brother Groves, ever a humble man, looked at us and said, "I pray for you? I should ask you to pray for me!"

But the Bible declares, *"...the lesser is blessed by the greater"* (Hebrews 7:7 – New American Standard Version). So, I insisted that he pray for us. Rev Groves then laid his hands upon our heads and prayed for us with all the faith and the fire that blazed in his heart. When he was finished, I knew that God had imparted something into my life. I had received some of the Fire of that old generation that had experienced Pentecost before us. This was one of the significant spiritual "milestones" in my life.

In Eastern cultures, we learn to honor, serve, and show respect to those older or greater than us. It is deeply ingrained in our psyche. In Western culture, most young men and women have this appalling habit of looking at themselves as "equal" to men of God who are older than them in age or in ministry. They treat them and address them with such familiarity that they miss out on what God wants to impart into their lives through these men who have walked with God much longer than they have. That is why these days we see more fiery faith-filled men rising up in Eastern cultures, where people understand honor, service, and respect much more than people do in Western countries.

Familiarity breeds contempt, but honor, service, and respect bring Fire and Anointing. We are all equally loved by God; but then, there are degrees and levels of anointing and of positions in ministry, and some of the things that God uses to take us to the next level are the principles of honor, service and respect. We must therefore honor, respect, and serve those who are senior to us in the ministry of the Gospel. This is a principle of utmost importance.

Jesus has paid the total price for people to be healed, but there is a dimension where those of us who desire to be used by God also have a price to pay. There is no power without sacrifice, no Glory without the Cross. To know His fullness, there is a price to pay.

119

Becoming men of faith and honor, rising to meet challenges, believing for souls to be saved, contending for people to be healed and to be delivered, walking in servanthood, seeking not to be exalted but in humility seeking to lay down our lives for others. In all this, keeping our eyes upon Jesus, upon the goal of our high calling in Him.

We have to humble ourselves, seek His face, and lay hold of God with all our hearts. We have to battle the fiery desires of our flesh, be quick to make things right when we stumble or fall, make sacrifices and lay down our lives to win the lost; be willing to decrease so that He, Christ Jesus, may increase. Whilst believing that God prospers us materially and blesses us with His abundance, we must also turn away from greed, from the love of money and the love of the things of this world; even to the point of sacrificing the material blessings that God bestows upon us in order to reach those who have never heard about Jesus.

This is what the ministry of the Gospel is all about.

Are you willing to deny yourself, take up the Cross, and follow the Savior?

Some years ago I was holding a crusade in Victoria Falls, Zimbabwe. My eldest son Immanuel was with me. He was 10 years old at the time. One morning, we decided to walk down to see the majestic Victoria Falls, one of the great natural wonders of this world. It is about a mile from the town of Victoria Falls to the actual falls. The sun was up and it was quite warm, so on our walk back to town we decided to stop for an ice cream.

There is a place opposite the entrance to the falls where tourist buses stop and one can buy snacks, drinks, and ice cream. The place was crowded with vendors and with European and American tourists. As we were buying ice cream from one of the vendors, a crowd surrounded us. A man came up to me and began to point at his ears and mouth, not saying anything. I did not understand what he wanted. The ice-cream vendor said to me, "Are you the pastor who is preaching at the big crusade?"

"Yes I am," I replied.

The vendor then said, "Pastor, this man was born deaf and mute and wants you to pray for him."

I looked around at the crowd surrounding me; at the white tourists from Europe and America. I felt intimidated because I knew exactly what they would think if they saw me pray for this deaf-mute man.

My heart sank; I did not "feel" anointed at that moment. I then said to the ice cream vendor, "Bring this man to the crusade tonight." I felt that the crusade, where I was "in control," was a "safer" atmosphere for me to pray for him. And then why not? After all, God was doing many miracles at the crusade every night!

This said, I bought Immanuel an ice cream and we walked away. We had only walked a few yards away from the tourist area when I heard the Holy Spirit speak to me very plainly and clearly, "What would Jesus do if He was here instead of you? Would He do as you did and tell the deaf-mute man to come to the crusade instead of praying for him right there?" I was struck with deep conviction. Then the Lord spoke again, "Look at your little son standing next to you. He is watching you. Do you want your son to believe in a Jesus who only does miracles in crusade services? What kind of legacy do you want to leave with

121

him when you leave this world; a legacy of Faith and Fire or a legacy of unbelief?"

I looked at the innocent face of my little boy and realized what the Holy Spirit was saying at that moment. What kind of spiritual legacy was I going to leave him? A legacy of faith in the power of an Almighty God, or a legacy of religious doubt and unbelief?

Our children look up to us. Not only at the things we say, but also at the things we do. I did not want to be a bad example to him. At the same time, I did not "feel" any "faith" or "anointing" and was very reticent to step out. I felt reluctant and afraid.

Then it struck me. What do my feelings have to do with it anyway? What does it matter how I "feel" or don't "feel"? This is not about me; it is about Jesus. No matter what I "feel," I should never let my "feelings" of faith or lack thereof become factors in this matter.

Faith is not about how I "feel." It is about Jesus, about His Word, and about Him keeping His Word. I should never ask myself how I "feel" but should always do what God says in His Word. What God said in His Word about that particular situation that I found myself in was, "... *they shall lay their hands upon the sick and they shall recover*" (Mark 16:18)!

As I stood there with these thoughts coursing through my mind, Immanuel asked, "Dad, why are we just standing here and doing nothing?"

I then looked at him again. I was not going to fail him. God's Word said, "...*they shall lay their hands upon the sick and they shall recover!*" I knew what I would do.

I said to Immanuel, "Let us go back and find that deaf-mute man."

We went back. We looked around, found him, and took him outside the crowd. I put my fingers in his deaf ears and prayed for him in the Mighty Name of our Lord Jesus Christ; the Name that is above every name, the Name that never fails.

In an instant the man was healed. His face broke into a big smile. He could hear! He also began to repeat the words that I spoke into his ears.

We thanked God for His mercy, and we started to walk away from there towards the town. I looked at Immanuel. He was quiet and reflective at first, and then he looked at me with a big smile and said loudly and full of enthusiasm, "Dad, Jesus is always bigger than the devil!"

Now THAT made my day! It was a priceless moment that I shall always cherish. I kissed him and looked away so that he would not be able to see my tears.

We who are Saved and Baptized with the Holy Ghost and with Fire have not inherited ashes, but Fire – Pentecostal Fire. The same Fire that fell on the day of Pentecost has been passed down to us through 2000 years of history. Jesus Christ has not changed; He is the same today. The Gospel has not changed. The Word of God has not changed. The Power of the Holy Ghost has not diminished. It is our right, our heritage, to believe God's Word; to act and to stand upon His Word, knowing that He shall always confirm it by bringing it to pass. It is our right to preach the Gospel and to expect God to confirm the Gospel message with signs following.

It is our right to walk in His Presence, to walk in the miraculous; to know that our Lord Jesus is still the same yesterday, today and for ever!

This is the priceless heritage passed down to us through the ages. We are treading the ground where our Lord Jesus Himself once trod. We are walking the blood-stained paths of glory where the saints of old once trod.

We have received abundant Grace, and we have received Fire!

What a wonderful legacy of faith that we can pass on to the next generation!

What a mighty God we serve! Hallelujah to Jesus for ever!

DO YOU WANT JESUS CHRIST IN YOUR LIFE?

DO YOU WANT HIM TO HEAL YOU?

"Surely he hath borne our griefs (diseases), and carried our sorrows (pains): yet we did esteem him stricken, smitten of God, and afflicted. But he was wounded for our transgressions, he was bruised for our iniquities: the chastisement of our peace was upon him; and with his stripes we are healed."
Isaiah 53:4-5

"Bless the LORD, O my soul: and all that is within me, bless his holy name. Bless the LORD, O my soul, and forget not all his benefits: Who forgiveth all thine iniquities; who healeth all thy diseases; Who redeemeth thy life from destruction; who crowneth thee with lovingkindness and tender mercies."
Psalm 103: 1-4

The Lord Jesus has already borne all of your diseases, pains, and infirmities upon Himself. You can now cast all your sins and diseases upon Him. Ask Jesus to touch you right now and receive His saving and healing power into your life, NOW!

Now, pray this prayer with me,

"Dear Lord Jesus, I thank you that when you suffered upon the whipping post and died upon the cross of Calvary you took all my sins, diseases, pains, and infirmities upon yourself. I, therefore, give you all my sins, diseases, pains, and infirmities and receive life and healing from you into my heart, mind, soul, and body. Lord Jesus, I give my heart, my mind, and my body to you. Thank you for touching me!

Every disease and every devil, hear this now! My body belongs to Jesus, and I command you to let go of me. Leave me now, in the Name of Jesus!

I cover myself with the Blood of Jesus! My body is healed because of Jesus! I belong to Jesus! Amen!"

Now rejoice and thank God every day of your life. Give yourself wholly to Jesus; walk with Him every single day of your life. Live close to Him, build yourself up, and live in the Word of God, and you shall see how the Blessings of God shall abound in your life!

God Bless you!

In Christ Jesus,

Christopher Alam

ABOUT THE AUTHOR

The author, Christopher Alam, lives in Lancaster, Pennsylvania with his wife, Britta, and their three children. They are graduates of RHEMA Bible Training Center in Broken Arrow, Oklahoma. Christopher is an Ordained Minister of the General Council of the Assemblies of God.

Christopher was born a Muslim and received Jesus Christ in 1975. After enduring much persecution including spending almost an entire year in prison for preaching the Gospel, Christopher was threatened with execution. After this he escaped and went to Sweden as a refugee where he was granted political asylum. There, in church, he met Swedish-born Britta.

You can read Christopher's story in his exciting book, "Out of Islam."

Christopher and Britta are the founders of Dynamis World Ministries, a worldwide missions organization with its headquarters in Lancaster, and with missions bases and offices in Sweden, Zimbabwe and in a closed country in Southeast Asia. They hold large open-air crusades, train pastors, plant churches, provide humanitarian relief, publish literature, and train church-planters at their church-planting school. They have preached the Gospel of Jesus Christ in over 70 nations. Signs and wonders follow the preaching of the Gospel and they have seen millions of people come to Christ in their crusades. Over a thousand churches have been started through their ministry worldwide.

Christopher is in much demand as a speaker in churches and conferences worldwide.

If you would like to contact Christopher and Britta or are interested in becoming a partner of Dynamis World Ministries, please write to:

Christopher and Britta Alam
Dynamis World Ministries
2384 New Holland Pike
Lancaster, PA 17601 USA
Tel: +1-717-656-0362
E-mail: info@pentecostalfire.com
www.pentecostalfire.com

Visit the ministry website to get more detailed information about the ministry. At the website, you can also read back copies of the monthly newsletter "Testimonies of Fire," download Christopher Alam's teaching messages for FREE, watch miracle videos, send in prayer requests, or make online financial contributions to the ministry.

JESUS PURCHASED THESE SOULS WITH HIS

WILL YOU HARVEST THEM?

Sponsor a Crusade

PURCHASED BY THE BLOOD

We know that money can never purchase a soul. Souls are only purchased by the precious Blood of Jesus. However, God has planned that through the preaching of the Gospel, these souls that Jesus purchased with His Blood can be harvested for His Kingdom.

CRUSADE EXPENSES

Crusade expenses include the following: advertising and publicity; travel costs, which covers Christopher's travel to Africa, as well as transporting our trucks and twenty-two tons of equipment to the crusade venue; housing and provisions for Christopher and our Africa Team while they are on the field during the Mobile Bible School and crusade(s); and follow-up materials, including various books and the Gospel of John.

CRUSADE BUDGET

In recent years, we have seen over a million people come to Jesus through our crusades annually. Our budget per crusade is $25,000, and a double crusade, or two back-to-back crusades, is $35,000.

SPONSOR A CRUSADE

Prayerfully consider making an investment with your business, or team up with your church, school, small group, or family to sponsor a crusade. Ask God to lead you and give you creative ideas to raise money to support the harvest of these precious souls!

If the Lord is leading you to sponsor a crusade, visit our website at *www.pentecostalfire.com* to make a secure online donation or send a check payable to *Dynamis World Ministries* to 2384 New Holland Pike, Lancaster, PA 17601 USA.